THE MYTH OF THE PERFECT MOTHER

THE MYTH OF THE
PERFECT MOTHER

Rethinking the Spirituality of Women

CARLA BARNHILL

BakerBooks
Grand Rapids, Michigan

© 2004 by Carla Barnhill

Published by Baker Books
a division of Baker Publishing Group
P.O. Box 6287, Grand Rapids, MI 49516-6287
www.bakerbooks.com

Printed in the United States of America

Library of Congress Cataloging-in-Publication Data
Barnhill, Carla.
    The myth of the perfect mother : rethinking the spirituality of women / Carla Barnhill.
        p.   cm.
    Includes bibliographical references.
    ISBN 0-8010-6466-X (pbk.)
    1. Mothers—Religious life. 2. Women—Religious life. 3. Spirituality. I. Title.
BV4529.18.B38 2004
248.8′431—dc22   2004009756

CONTENTS

INTRODUCTION

My life is in the hands of a two-year-old.

Take this morning, for example. I'm trying to meet a deadline for work, so I'm sitting in my basement, laptop up and running. My daughter is at school, and I've just laid my son down for the nap he's thinking about giving up. I have big hopes that today he'll sleep for three hours like he did yesterday and I'll be able to get some real work done.

But he's not asleep. I hear him on the monitor, jabbering to his stuffed elephant, singing to himself, and occasionally yelling for his sister (she's recently begun to get him out of his bed in the morning; I haven't asked her to do this, but it lets me stay in bed for about two extra minutes, so I'm not complaining).

Since he sounds content, I decide to let him hang out in his bed for a while, but then he starts to cry in earnest, and I wonder if he's gotten his leg stuck in the crib slats again. So I head to his room and find him lying down, probably on his way to dreamland. But of course, he lifts his head and sees me, so any thoughts of sleeping he might have had are gone.

I could try to write while he plays nearby, but he's at the age where I can't even get a spoon in the dishwasher without his "help." The genius I was sure to pour out today will have to wait. I log off and we head to Target.

This is motherhood for me. It's going through a day without much control over what happens when. It's adjusting my plans to meet the needs of my children. It's getting up way before my body wants to and being instantly required to think on my feet.

Not that those are always bad things. I don't mind having an excuse not to get my work done; believe me, I'd rather push trains around a green plastic mountain with Isaac than edit an article about circumcision. And I love to follow the whims of my kids; their ideas are invariably more interesting than mine. The sleep thing? Well, I'm still trying to find the upside of being awake at 7:00 a.m.

But the hard truth is, I have a job, and if I miss my deadlines, my nice work-at-home situation will come to a swift end. There are days—many days—when I truly cannot fit a shower into my schedule. Some afternoons I am very, very tired and would love a nap. I'd love to read a book or even a magazine for an hour straight. I'd love to have an uninterrupted conversation with a friend. I'd love to have my house stay clean for more than twenty minutes. I'd love to have someone tend to me when I feel sick. As much as I try to be a fabulous mother who sees the bigger picture, there are times when motherhood feels like a burden.

Now, I love my children more than life. If I do say so myself, God has graced me with two of the most spectacular children ever created. They are beautiful, delightful, funny, sweet, and bright, and every night I thank God that

I've had another day in their presence. My feelings about motherhood have nothing to do with who they are or the way they behave. I'm sure of this because so many other mothers with equally fabulous children have told me they experience many of these same feelings.

Lots of books address this "secret" life of mothers. They talk about the weariness, the loss of a sense of self, the physical and emotional toll of motherhood. Because of books such as Naomi Wolf's *Misconceptions* and Harriet Learner's *The Mother Dance,* those issues aren't really so secret anymore. Most of us feel reasonably free to admit that we get worn out by our children, that we crave time alone and a decent night's sleep. But I'm not writing this book to talk about how tired moms are. I'm writing this book because of Andrea Yates.

On June 20, 2001, Andrea Yates, a thirty-seven-year-old wife and mother, drowned her five children in the bathtub, one at a time. In March of 2002, she was convicted of three counts of first-degree murder and sentenced to life in prison. During her trial, it came out that she had been severely depressed for years. She had tried to kill herself in 1999. She had been hospitalized for severe depression on three separate occasions, the most recent time being only three months before she killed her children.

As I read about the trial, it seemed so clear to me that this horrific tragedy was completely preventable. Clearly, this was a very, very sick woman. One of the psychiatrists who assessed her said Yates was among the five sickest patients she'd ever worked with. The doctor who did Yates's intake evaluation at the last psychiatric hospital said Yates was a "shell" of a human being and was so obviously sick that she couldn't understand why Andrea's family had waited so long to bring her to the hospital.

Andrea Yates's best friend testified that she had begged Andrea's husband, Russell, to get help for Andrea. Andrea Yates's mother and brothers were publicly critical of Russell and held him partly to blame for the deaths of the children, calling him "unemotional" and charging that he did not help with the parenting.

I don't know what life was like for Andrea and Russell Yates. But I do know that there were numerous signs of this mother's slide into a frightening abyss of depression and psychosis that no one took seriously enough to act on. I know that Andrea Yates was a Christian woman with a church family, a biological family, and a husband, all of whom she believed she was failing with her perceived inadequacies as a mother. I know that Andrea Yates herself told authorities she felt she could never talk to anyone about the feelings of loneliness, uselessness, and shame that eventually overwhelmed her. I also know that on some level, every mother understands Andrea Yates.

Andrea Yates represents the extreme end of the spectrum of physical, emotional, and spiritual changes that women experience when they become mothers. The vast majority of us will never hurt our children, but nearly every one of us will think about it.

This book is about what happens when the reality of a woman's experience doesn't match up with the messages we get about motherhood. It's about what happens when we discover that this role we've been told will be one of God's greatest blessings instead feels frustrating and defeating. It's about the real lives of Christian mothers and how they deal with the emotional and spiritual toll of motherhood.

My goal isn't to bad-mouth motherhood or the church. It's to open up a conversation about the expectations placed on Christian mothers and how those expectations keep women from finding out who God created them to be. My hope is that those who read this book will begin to strip away the false expectations of Christian culture so mothers can reclaim their personhood in Christ and parent their children without fear or guilt. I would be thrilled if pastors read this book and started thinking about the women in their churches who are impacted by these messages about motherhood and family. I would die a happy woman if a group of mothers read this book and started really talking about their experiences as moms and finding ways to support each other as sisters in Christ, as women who want to know God, and as people just trying to find their way on the incredible journey of faith.

1

The Cult of the Family

See if any of this sounds familiar: The "good" Christian mother is one who is always loving, always patient, always happy, always ready to serve her family. She finds tremendous satisfaction in being a mother. She is devoted to her children and gladly puts her own needs aside to meet theirs. She keeps her house clean, her children organized, and her husband happy, all with the joyful heart of a servant.

Because of her love and devotion to her children, they are clean, obedient, well behaved, and respectful. Because she models Christ's attitude of service and selflessness, her children learn to share, to cooperate, to be other-centered, to give with glad hearts. You can tell she is a good mother because her kids love to sing praise songs, watch Veggie-Tales videos, and say their prayers. They eagerly participate in family devotions because their mother plans interesting, creative activities that bring biblical truths to life. As teenagers, these children become leaders in their youth groups and stand strong in the face of peer pressure. They are testaments to their mother's sacrificial love and truly godly parenting.

Does your life look like that? Mine either.

Being a mother is an exhilarating experience, one that brings life to corners of our hearts we didn't know were there—the author Susan Cheever says it's like walking into the sunlight after living our whole lives by starlight. But deep inside, women with children also know that motherhood comes with a tremendous cost. I don't just mean the lack of sleep or the lack of alone time. I'm talking about the unending burden of a role that has been both undervalued and overly romanticized by our culture.

Christian women in particular grow up being taught that motherhood will somehow complete us, that in motherhood, we will find the culmination of all our hopes and dreams. We hear countless sermons on the family and how what we do as parents will indelibly shape the faith of our children. We read the stacks of parenting books that reduce raising children to a simple formula of prayer, Bible study, and firm discipline.

As a result, women come to believe their ultimate worth is found in motherhood, not in their relationship with God. They come to believe that their real contribution to the world is to raise perfect children, not to explore their gifts in the context of the greater community. It's this false perception that leads women to struggle with the incongruity between who God created them to be and who the church tells them they should be. This mentality is the natural outgrowth of what I call the cult of the family.

Life in the Cult

When I say there exists a cultlike mentality in the Christian world, I'm suggesting that our churches have elevated the family to a position of importance that is out of sync with the call of the gospel. We have been led to believe that the family is more important than the broader community, that protecting our children from the evils of secular culture is more important than bringing God's love into that culture. We have been allowed to barricade ourselves from being salt and light to the world by hiding behind what's "best for our children."

For women, those messages translate directly to expectations about our role in building families that model Christian ideals. We've been brainwashed into believing that there is an ideal model of the Christian family and therefore an ideal model of Christian motherhood. We believe that the Bible somehow mandates a certain style of parenting, a certain set of behaviors for all mothers everywhere.

However, much of what we assign to our ideal of the Christian mother actually echoes the cultural model of motherhood that has developed in the United States over the past two centuries.[1] The inbreeding of the secular assumptions about motherhood and the religious understanding of the family has created a mind-set that pulls Christian women away from the heart of the gospel and instead binds us up with a restrictive set of expectations about who we are, what we're here for, and how God can use us in the world.

There's nothing inherently wrong with the Christian ideals of motherhood—that we be loving and patient and kind. They are perfectly noble and certainly worth aspiring to. What's troublesome about this view is that it bases a woman's worth on her success as a mother, not on her

15

value as a child of God. And it's nearly impossible to define "successful" motherhood.

In reality, few women feel even remotely successful as mothers. The real toll of motherhood often blindsides women who grow up believing that becoming a mother will be the greatest thing ever to happen to them. Instead of floating along in a sea of motherly bliss, many of us find ourselves conflicted, depressed, guilt-ridden, lonely, even suicidal. Sadly, when those feelings begin to creep in, the last place many of us feel comfortable talking about them is in our churches.

As the editor of *Christian Parenting Today* magazine, I write a regular column. Not long ago, I based my column on some of the issues raised in this book. After opening up a bit about my sense that we have a tendency to put the call of motherhood above the call of the gospel, I wrote, "I feel like I've stopped serving the kingdom because I'm too busy serving my family." That one sentence generated more angry mail than anything else we've run in the magazine, with the sole exception of a piece on the Harry Potter books.

Even though my editor's note made it clear that I was talking about my own feelings, and being pretty vulnerable about it at that, only one reader offered to pray for me. The rest offered only judgment and shock that I would dare to feel the way I did.

The Golden Age

While motherhood is indeed a blessing, it borders on idolatry for the church to hold motherhood up as a woman's most sacred calling, particularly because this idea is based not on the Bible but on a secular model of a woman's role. Theologian Gilbert Bilezikian says, "The Scriptures repeatedly warn believers against the subtle danger of uncritically adopting prevalent cultural concepts and worldly practices. Christians are commanded to examine their assumptions in the light of God's Word and, should they do so, they are given the promise that they will be able to discover His divine will. 'Do not be conformed to this world but be transformed by the renewal of your mind. Then you will be able to test and verify what God's will is, His good, pleasing, and perfect will' (Rom. 12:2)."[2] And yet, this "uncritical" adoption of the secular view of women is exactly what's happened in the evangelical culture.

For many evangelicals, the 1950s are the epitome of all that is good and holy in family life—Dad at work, Mom at home, the three-bedroom house with a yard, a dog, a station wagon, and two happy, smiling children. This is the family we are trying to live up to.

The truth is, the model '50s family is an anomaly in the history of the family (not to mention the history of the church). Consider this comment from historian Elaine Tyler May:

Observers often point to the 1950s as the last gasp of time-honored family life before the sixties generation made a major break from the past. But the comparison is short-sighted. In many ways, the youth of the sixties resembled their grandparents, who came of age in the first decades of the twentieth century. Like many of their baby-boom grandchildren, the grandparents had challenged the sexual norms of their day, pushed the divorce rate up and the birthrate down, and created a unique youth culture, complete with music, dancing, movies, and other new forms of urban amusements. They also behaved in similar ways politically, developing a powerful feminist movement, strong grassroots activism on behalf of social justice, and a proliferation of radical movements to challenge the status quo. It is the generation in between—with its strong domestic ideology, pervasive consensus politics, and peculiar demographic behavior—that stands out as different.[3]

It's also a mistake to assume that the "traditional" family model we associate with the '50s had anything to do with conservative Christian values or a generation of people who finally got family "right." In truth, our modern understanding of family owes more to Richard Nixon than to the church.

In an effort to make the American way of life appear superior to Communism, mid-century American political leaders promoted the idea that in America, every family could own its own home, that jobs were so plentiful and lucrative women had the luxury of staying home, that capitalism allowed every family to own a car and a washing machine. The middle-class, suburban family was created to make America look good.[4] May notes, "For Nixon, American superiority rested on the ideal of the suburban home, complete with modern appliances and distinct gender roles for family members. He proclaimed that the 'model' home, with a male breadwinner and a full-time female homemaker, adorned with a wide array of consumer goods, represented the essence of American freedom."[5]

The same trappings—the house, the yard, the family itself—have been incorporated in the evangelical assumptions about women (and to some degree men, but that's a whole other conversation). We have translated the '50s model of the perfect American family to the model of the perfect Christian family. In doing so, we have taken away a woman's ability to follow God's leading in her life and replaced it with a kind of bondage to an ideal that isn't consistent with the call of Scripture.

A Divine Calling

Many Christian women consider motherhood a calling. In some ways, that's an appropriate word for it; for a woman to deal with all the demands of motherhood, it's probably helpful to feel as though she's been led into this role in some way. But it's a grave mistake for us to casually name motherhood a divine calling.

One of the most life-changing sermons I ever heard was about the idea of God calling people to a particular kind of life. The pastor explained that Scripture actually only refers to a few people being "called" to a specific purpose (think of Moses and the burning bush). The rest of us are told to "act justly and to love mercy and to walk humbly with [our] God" (Micah 6:8). That directive is about our character, about how we are to live in the world.

Naturally, our character is to infect all that we do, whether we're mothers or brain surgeons (or both). But God does not call most of us to a certain role. I certainly didn't become a mother because I felt "called" to it. I became a mother because it seemed like the thing to do after being married for a few years. I liked the idea, and I knew we'd make decent parents. I wanted my mom and dad to enjoy grandchildren. Did I sense God telling me that I had to have kids? Nope.

I struggle with this idea of motherhood as a calling primarily because of the picture of God it creates. If God calls women to motherhood, then why isn't God calling my friend Elizabeth who is going through daily hormone shots in the stomach in an effort to have a child? Or my friend Dana who has suffered five miscarriages? Or my friend Jenae whose child was stillborn? Would God really put an intense desire for children into a woman's heart and then deny her the "call" to have them? While I believe every child is a divine gift, and that God is present and will bring good out of the situations mentioned here, there is simply no biblical evidence to suggest that God sits on a throne and decides who should get children and who shouldn't.

Thinking of motherhood as a calling also creates the impression that caring for children is a woman's primary life function and demands the exclusion of any other kind of "calling." A woman's worth as a child of God then becomes lost under the crushing responsibility of mothering. When a woman is told to focus all her energies on growing her children, she often loses her ability to allow her heavenly Father to grow her. Worst of all, there is tremendous pressure for women to do what's best for their families even if it comes into conflict with the call of the gospel.

In too many cases, Christian parenting books use language that suggests that passing on our faith to our children—not the "next generation" but the two or three children who live in our homes—is the single highest priority for parents, that nothing even comes close to it in importance. I recognize that the hyperbole is intended to push parents to take our role seriously. But most of us already do. We don't need an expert to tell us to pour ourselves into our children. In fact, we often need Christian parenting experts to help us do exactly the opposite.

Over and over, Christian parenting experts tell us to let nothing get in the way of the spiritual development of our children. And while that's certainly a worthy ideal, the strong language that insists we put our children above all else runs contrary to the words of Jesus, who warned against loving our children more than we love God (Matt. 10:37). In fact, there might be times, Jesus suggests, when the gospel will call us to live in a way that makes us put our children second.

How many of us might have felt a pull to serve the kingdom in the inner city or on the mission field but resisted because it would put our own children at risk? In her wonderful book *Gender and Grace,* Christian psychologist Mary Stewart Van Leeuwen reminds us that Jesus "affirms parenthood as an important calling for both men and women and a role that deserves respect from children. But he does not allow these roles to take precedence over the kingdom of God. He does not allow them to be idolized."[6] It seems to me that telling parents that nothing is as important is creating exactly that kind of idolatry.

I have to admit that I suffer from this tension between doing what's best for my children and serving the broader kingdom. A private Christian school is opening up in a poor neighborhood not far from where we live. One night as I drove by I thought, *I hope that school makes it. I hope some solid families will send their kids there so the school can thrive.* But if I really care, I ought to enroll my own children in this school. If I believe it's a worthy idea, I should commit to supporting it. And yet I'm not willing to send my children into this neighborhood. I'm not willing to "risk" their education, their safety, their well-being in order to serve this neighborhood. In other words, I have allowed my children to be more important than God's tug on my heart.

That's exactly what a cult does. It focuses our attention on something else so the truth of the gospel gets lost or mishandled for some other purpose. It pulls people away from God's truth toward an alternate "truth."

Many women believe that being a mother *is* serving the kingdom, that there is no conflict here because we are doing what God wants us to be doing and God understands that we can't do more. While I agree that motherhood is a tremendous blessing, I don't believe it is the sum total of what God expects of me. To me, the Bible is pretty clear

21

that I was created to bring God's love to the world (Matt. 28:19), to love and serve God with my whole being (Deut. 6:5), and to do all I can to live my life in the way of Jesus (Eph. 5:1–2). Anything that distracts me from that, even if it's something very, very good, is distracting me from moving toward God.

The Slippery Slope

The cult of the family creates a culture in which women are not allowed to feel anything but good about motherhood because it is the best God has for them. We are not allowed to want something in our lives in addition to motherhood because this role should be enough. And we are not allowed to suggest that motherhood is anything but a blessing because to do so is to denigrate the most wondrous calling God can give a woman.

When we published my column about serving the kingdom, I received a letter from a woman who summarized the evangelical view of motherhood. Her letter sheds light on the many ways in which the cult of the family creates a dangerous ideology for women. Let me show you what I mean by taking a look at her basic argument:

Being a mother is all about service. I don't know of a loving, caring mother anywhere who fails to serve her children even when it doesn't feel good. We get up in the middle of the night to serve our children. We leave our jobs or spend only minutes a day with our husbands to serve our children. We run ourselves ragged to serve our children.

Women have a God-given urge to give and serve and sacrifice for our children. I don't believe that Christian women have a problem with not serving enough. If anything, we have confused servanthood with servitude; we allow our own needs to go unmet even when doing so impacts our children in a negative way. How good a mom can I be when I'm tired, stressed, and desperate to talk about something besides who threw up at kindergarten?

Motherhood is about a whole lot more than serving. It's about helping our children discover who God created them to be. It's about nurturing them, loving them, teaching them, caring for them, and then sending them out into the world to use their gifts in God's service. Sometimes it's about *not* serving them so they can learn that the needs of other people are at least as important as their own.

We show our love of Christ through our work in the home. There is nothing, I mean nothing, biblical about housework. The Bible never commands women to clean the house, do the laundry, or cook dinner. In Luke 10:41–42, we read that Martha's focus on housework was preventing her from focusing on Jesus. He told her that knowing him and listening to him was far more important than washing dishes. Most Christian women get so bogged down by their efforts to keep up appearances and hold their households together that they truly do miss out on their relationships with God, not to mention the families they are trying to serve.

We are commanded to care for our husbands and children. There is no such command anywhere in Scripture. Author J. Lee Grady says, "We often quote Titus 2:4 which says, 'Encourage the young women to love their husbands, to love their children, to be sensible, pure, workers at home.' Then we twist this verse to say that God requires all women to fit into the cookie-cutter mold of the full-time Christian housewife."[7] The thinking that leads this reader to believe her purpose is to serve her family suggests that no matter who we are prior to marriage and motherhood, all of that is irrelevant in the face of this so-called command to take care of our families. And once again, I've found that most Christian mothers get ground down because they care and serve to the point of exhaustion. The problem isn't that we don't serve enough, it's that we serve too much.

The woman ended her letter with this statement: "I think our goal as mothers should be to make our children our greatest contribution to the kingdom of God. The children we are raising could become the last prophet, the preacher who leads millions to Christ, the doctor who finds a cure for AIDS, or any number of great things." I agree that it is a profound honor to raise two human beings, to help them discover who God created them to be. They will indeed be part of the legacy I leave in this world. But I also have a responsibility to raise them to see themselves as part of something bigger than our family. They need to see in me the desire to follow God's leading, even if it isn't the best thing for them at the time. They need to see me choosing to serve others because God tells me to, not because I'm legally obligated to. I fully believe that God can lead anyone into a life of service no matter how they are raised, but I think my children will be a whole lot more open to hearing God's voice if they see both of their parents striving to do the same.

This mother clearly believes that women serve God's kingdom in motherhood. She is passionate about mother-hood being a godly use of a woman's time and energy. And yet she doesn't see the irony of finding comfort in knowing we can raise the next generation of prophets or preachers. In her desire for me to play my part in helping my children go on to serve the kingdom, she never mentions that one of them might do so as a mother.

2

THE GOOD CHRISTIAN MOTHER

I often joke that one of my motivations as a mother is the "stupid mom" factor. I try not to do anything that, if it appeared in a newspaper headline, would have other mothers thinking, "What a stupid mom!" So I've never run to the grocery store two blocks away while my baby is asleep, even though it would be so easy to be there and back in ten minutes (Baby Dies in House Fire. Mother at Store). I've never left my kids in the car while I run in to the ATM . . . okay, once, but I could see the car the whole time and it was freezing outside (Children Stolen while Mother Gets Cash). The shame and guilt that would come from doing something really dumb is enough to keep me from doing it.

Because the church holds up the family as sacrosanct, it follows that mothers, who are expected to keep the family humming along, are the lynchpin of the cult of the family.

There is, therefore, tremendous pressure for mothers to raise great Christian kids for the sake of the church. It's ironic that the pervading pressure to be a perfect mother—which I think is intended to make women feel like their work as moms is important—actually defeats mothers at every turn.

As research for this book, I sent out a survey to more than fifty women I know (and a few I don't) to find out about their experiences as moms. Nearly every one of the evangelical women I surveyed has felt as if she's failed as a mother in some sense. Maggie, the mother of a three-year-old, says, "There's a lot of pressure to be perfect, like you aren't allowed to have bad days or say anything negative about motherhood. There's a lot of guilt about whether you're doing things correctly. There also seems to be a feeling that moms should sacrifice their own selves/desires/needs/goals for those of their children and that you should feel guilty about taking time away from your kids."

Much of that guilt comes from entering motherhood with a set of expectations about what it means to be a mother only to find those expectations dashed within the first week of life as a mom. Martha, the mother of two, told me, "The church has sent the message that bearing children is a woman's penultimate role, the culmination of everything a woman can hope to achieve. There's also the sense that my family should be loving, patient, kind, gentle, successful, and well behaved. If they aren't, I'm to blame. At the same time, there's a message that my success as a parent is a crucial part of my personhood."

For Martha, these ideals were crushed early on. Her first child was born with severe gastroesophageal reflux, which meant that her baby vomited often and had a hard time nursing. Martha says, "I struggled for weeks to nurse her because I knew the hot button it was to bottle feed among the women in my Christian circle. This forced nursing led to discomfort for my daughter and anxiety, marital stress, depression, and suicidal thoughts for me. I felt like such a failure because I seemingly could not care for, satiate, or comfort my baby—ever."

Erin is the mother of three boys, two of whom are now adults. She says, "In the early years of my two oldest sons' lives, I was devastated when they 'acted up' in public. I often felt pretty much like a failure."

Another woman, Joanne, said that when her eighteen-year-old stepdaughter started down the path of a prodigal, her family found themselves "facing problems I'd always felt Christian families shouldn't face. Many people insinuate that our daughter's rebellion is totally our fault."

When Cecilia's teenage son got into trouble with the police, Cecilia found that people at her church were less interested in how their family was coping than in blaming her. She says, "What your children do or don't do has a direct bearing on how you are perceived in the church. People judge with little or no information. Their perceptions are based on behavior, not facts."

In each of these cases, the church became not a place of support and encouragement but a place of judgment and blame. The message these women received is much like the parenting propaganda developed in the secular culture over the last few centuries: Your child is a blank slate upon which your parenting will make a mark. The mark you make will either create a good child or a bad child. (I'll talk more about the idea of the child as a blank slate in chapter 3.)

I don't know about you, but I fail to live up to the expectation of a "good" Christian mother at least once an hour. I have yelled at my daughter when she really wasn't doing anything other than being six. I have raised my voice at my two-year-old because he wouldn't stop crying. I have shamed and scolded my kids when they didn't deserve it and failed to discipline them when they did.

One morning I let my son stay in his bed wide awake for an extra twenty minutes because I was so-o-o tired and didn't want to get out of bed yet. In one of those priceless moments of divine justice, when I finally went to get him he was absolutely covered in poop—his legs, his arms, his crib, his pillow. Even after putting him in the tub, I had to scrape the dried poop off with my fingernails (Child Digests Own Feces while Lazy Mother Lies in Bed). Believe me, I get him up right away now.

Just this week, my husband was in our basement, I was busy in the kitchen, and our daughter was upstairs playing, I assumed, with her brother. Then came a knock at the door. There was my neighbor Julie holding my son in her arms. He'd wandered outside, ACROSS THE STREET! and into another neighbor's yard. We didn't even know he was gone (Boy Runs Away while Stupid, Stupid, Stupid, Distracted, Stupid Mother Washes Dishes).

We have also made plenty of parenting decisions that we feel good about but that other Christians would vehemently disagree with. We don't spank. Sometimes our kids sleep with us. I nursed both kids for a year and sometimes fed them on demand, sometimes on a schedule. I worked full-time until my daughter was four. Our son didn't sleep through the night until he was nine months old, and only then did we decide to let him "cry it out" for a few nights. Our daughter goes to public school, and our son will too. We often watch *The Simpsons* with our kids. They both take communion. Both children were baptized as babies, not as believers. I fully intend to read the Harry Potter books with them when they are older.

If any of those things convince you I'm not a good mother or a good Christian, you're not alone. My guess, though, is that every one of us has a few parenting skeletons in our closets, choices we've made we might feel are fine but that we don't tell our church friends about because we know they'd think less of us.

It concerns me that, as I've talked about this project with women, so many of them have told me that this is a needed book. They have felt as if there are parenting issues they can't talk about in their churches because the evangelical culture tends to promote this idea that godly families don't have issues. They have felt as if their loneliness is seen as a character flaw, not a genuine need for deeper relationships. They have been told that if they aren't adhering to a particular style of parenting, they are failing their children. They have felt as if any acknowledgment that motherhood can suck the life out of a person is met with the admonition that a woman should be happy for the chance to serve her family. Almost every woman I surveyed has felt these things to some degree, but only a few have ever talked about these feelings with other moms.

Ellen has four children. She says, "I was not prepared for *not* feeling like apparently every other mom in history had felt—like mothering is the most wonderful thing on earth. Now I know that we've all felt like that, we just don't say so." Imagine the power we could give each other by being open about the challenges and defeating moments of motherhood. The failure we all feel at some point could vanish if we learned to show each other grace, encouragement, and honesty in the struggles we face as mothers.

The Profanity of Perfection

The idea that it's possible to be a "perfect" Christian mother is not only damaging to women who are desperately trying to do right by their children; it's also a perversion of our basic Christian belief in the saving power of Jesus. It's incredibly arrogant for us to believe that our human action is necessary for God to act in the lives of our children.

The Bible makes it quite clear that each of us is a unique creation of God (Psalm 139). Any mother who has brought home a baby who cries all the time or won't sleep or who refuses to take a bottle can tell you that even newborns have a personality all their own. Any mother of a prodigal can tell you that our children will make their own choices no matter how hard we worked to instill God's truth in them. Naturally, I believe that we parents have a little something to do with how our children turn out, but I also believe it's blasphemous to think God's ability to touch the hearts of my children is somehow dependent on my skill as a parent.

Think for a minute about other Christians you know. Now think about how many of them were raised in Christian homes. If your friends are like mine, probably a few became Christians after very difficult childhoods where God's name was spoken only in vain.

My friend Megan was sexually abused by her father. Her mother left the family to live with another man on the other side of the country. Her parents were Unitarians in their best moments and just plain pagan in their worst. And yet God lived in Megan just the same and has grown her into one of the most passionate, caring, joyful Christians I have ever known. The parenting she received could have ruined her, and indeed, the aftermath of her childhood has led to some painfully dark times in her life. But she has the faith to lead a Bible study for new Christians, to parent her children with incredible grace and love, and to boldly proclaim her love for Jesus to anyone within earshot.

It's also important to point out that there was a time when children were not even deemed capable of understanding things of faith. Historian Jan Lewis notes that as popular psychology grew to include the field of child development, "Evangelical views about youthful conversion built upon secular ones about the malleability of character, giving mothers a new responsibility. The work of redemption had to begin early, when a child was still in its mother's care, and, to the extent that evangelicals believed that the world had to be reclaimed individual by individual, the home became the main arena for conversions. . . . Mothers, thus, had it in their power to achieve not only the salvation of their children but also of the entire world."[1] Here again, our Christian framework has been influenced by secular culture. We have created a role for mothers based on science and psychology and passed it off as "God's way."

The idea that mothers are responsible for the spirituality of their children is cult thinking at its most profane. If it were possible for mothers to raise perfect children, we would have no need for Jesus. If it were possible for "good" parenting to keep children on the straight and narrow, there would be far fewer heartbroken mothers and fathers in our churches.

The truth is that each child is born with his or her own set of gifts and weaknesses. Every child will experience God in his or her own way. At the end of the day, the best we can hope for is that we haven't messed our kids up too badly. (One of the most disconcerting realizations I had as a new mom was that *I* was the one my daughter would be griping about with her friends or therapist one day: "My mom is so unfair!" "You think that's bad, wait till you hear what *my* mom said to me once." "My mom never showed me the kind of love I needed," and on and on.)

I certainly don't mean to imply that parents aren't important; Megan would tell you that her life would have been a whole lot easier if her parents had been Christians. There are several passages in the Bible that implore parents to be intentional about passing a heritage of faith on to their children. But when we place the full weight of raising God-fearing children in the hands of parents, we discount God's ability to reach a child without us.

Maybe I've freaked you out a little here. I do hope though that somewhere along the way, a light has gone on for you, one that has you rethinking your assumptions about what it means—and doesn't mean—to be a Christian mother. Even if you don't agree with me, the best result any author can hope for is for a book to open up conversations about an issue. If the ideas discussed so far don't ring true for you, that's fine. But I'd ask you to look around at the women in your church and search for those who seem worn down, listless, or at a loss for how to deal with the challenges of parenthood. Take one of them out for coffee—sans kids!—and find out how she's handling this stage in her life. Figure out what you can do to ease her load and commit to helping her get the rest and time she needs to live out the dreams God has placed in her heart. Support her as she seeks God's wisdom in her life, even if God leads her down a path that is very different from the one you're following.

A friend of mine told me about a woman he knows who was the stay-at-home mom of three kids, including one with cerebral palsy. Her children are now grown, and her special-needs son lives in a long-term care facility near her home. She and her husband have started graduate school together, earning advanced degrees in biomedical ethics. My friend Tony told me, "It's awesome that she took the things God put in her life and saw the bigger picture of what they could mean in terms of the kingdom." In the midst of the intense challenges of raising her children, she sensed that there had to be a grander purpose to her situation. She allowed her mothering to shape her into a person who is using her gifts to impact her culture. Rather than seeing her children as her sole contribution to the world, she has used her parenting experiences to effect broader change. The motherhood chapters of her life now inform the rest of her story.

How that kind of perspective plays out in your life is going to be up to you, but I would like to offer some thoughts. In order to break free of this cultlike thinking, we need to find out for ourselves what expectations we carry around. Think about your own view of motherhood. What is the "ideal" picture you're trying to live up to? Take a little time to decipher where that ideal came from, what has factored into how you see motherhood. Don't worry if you can't answer that question. One curious result of my survey is that nearly every woman knows what the false expectations are, but few can articulate where they came from. It's not as if pastors are standing in their pulpits telling women to homeschool (well, maybe some are) or that Christian women come right out and tell each other to stay home with their children (again, maybe some do), and yet we've gotten these messages in subtle ways. Perhaps you read a book that formed some of your thinking, or there was a woman in the church you grew up in who seemed to have it all together and became your image of a good mom. Maybe it's just the disapproval you sense when you make a parenting decision that doesn't jibe with your fellow Christian moms.

Once you have a better understanding of where your

expectations are coming from, you can start getting rid of those that come from our culture and replace them with real biblical truths about who God created you to be and how you can move toward *that* ideal in the midst of motherhood.

A Case Study

Willow Creek Community Church in South Barrington, Illinois, might not be everyone's cup of cappuccino; it's enormous, with thousands of people in attendance at any given service. As the forerunner of the "seeker" church movement, Willow Creek has been accused of watering down the gospel and not offering enough substance for more mature Christians.

Willow Creek also exemplifies market-driven ministry at its most extreme. Walking into Willow Creek is a little like walking into a mall at Christmastime. You look over the map, find the places you want to check out, hit the food court, and wait for the entertainment to begin. When it comes to programs, you want it, you'll find it. There are concerts and stores, books and brochures, classes and events for every imaginable niche of human being.

While some find this approach to ministry distasteful, I think Willow Creek does something other churches would be wise to try. They understand that people have layers of need. Just because someone is a teenager doesn't mean he or she won't be interested in service opportunites. Just because a person is poor doesn't mean he or she won't come to a class on creative worship. And just because someone is a mother doesn't mean she wouldn't like to learn more about living out her faith at her job.

I researched the women's ministry opportunities of several large churches. Most had at least one or two basic options for women. But I noticed that the kinds of classes offered at most churches reflected the idea that Christian women only want or need spiritual formation as it relates to a certain brand of motherhood.

All kinds of assumptions are made about who will come to these classes. Most churches offer something during a weekday morning and provide childcare for those who attend (which assumes the moms in the church are home during the day). Some offer classes at night, but usually without the childcare option (which assumes there is a dad at home to watch the kids). In many churches, the *only* women's ministry options are related to motherhood, which leaves childless women out in the cold.

Willow Creek breaks the mold by not only offering a huge range of options for women but by making it clear that women are welcome in nearly every class they have. Willow Creek has done a masterful job of providing small groups for executive women, mothers of preteens, women who work from home, women looking for work, women who want to study the Bible, and women who want to train for the mission field. They also offer childcare during a large number of their classes, so that no opportunity for spiritual formation is closed to a woman with children. They send the clear message that a woman is welcome to participate in the life of the church in any way in which she feels led, regardless of her maternal status.

Even the smallest church can take a page from the Willow Creek book. Imagine if churches treated women as Christians rather than as mothers. Imagine if Bible studies and prayer meetings and service projects were worked into a schedule that made it possible for every woman (and man) to participate. It could be as simple as providing childcare at all church functions, no matter how small, no matter the time of day. It could be as big as holding an open house (childcare provided!) for women to gather and talk about what their spiritual needs and gifts are and how the church can respond to those concerns. Maybe the moms of the church *will* want to get together for mutual support and encouragement, but maybe they'd rather hang out with older women who can mentor them as Christians or with childless women who share a passion for music or art. The idea is for churches to open their understanding of "women's ministry" to center on a woman's multifaceted spirituality, rather than on her stage of life.

3

THE MAKING OF A MYTH

I t's impossible to talk about our evangelical views of motherhood without having a firm understanding of the ways those views have been influenced by secular culture. That's because much of what evangelicals think of as the "Christian" ideal of motherhood is really based on cultural trends and secular ways of thinking rather than on biblical principles.

Motherhood in Early America

We tend to believe that motherhood has always been synonymous with love and care, but historians have noted that for early American women, not to mention contemporary women in nonindustrialized nations, motherhood was primarily thought of as a physical, not emotional or spiritual, undertaking. It's no wonder when you consider that once they were married, most seventeenth- and eighteenth-century women spent a good twenty to twenty-five years either pregnant or nursing. The physical toll was enormous and undoubtedly left women little energy for pursuits beyond meeting the basic physical needs of their children.

Because this was the reality of a woman's life, the ideal mother was one who met those physical needs well. A woman showed her attachment to her family by providing food, clothing, and shelter.[1] That is, when she wasn't also feeding the livestock, helping haul in the crops, grinding flour by hand, and washing her family's clothes in the creek.

While mothers in this era undoubtedly loved their children, in Puritan America, emotions were something to be feared. Love was suspect because it led to indulgence, which went against the grain of the Puritan ethos of restraint. Women were actually discouraged from expressing intense emotions for their children.[2]

The idea that motherhood involved more than giving birth and sustenance really began to develop in the mid-eighteenth century in conjunction with the American Revolution. Jan Lewis notes that, "The Revolutionary brew was seasoned by a variety of ingredients—republicanism, liberalism, evangelical Protestantism, sensationalist psychology—and just as each of these strands of thought would contribute to political thought, so too would they affect the conceptualization of family roles. . . . This transformation in political and familial thought would make room for a new ideal of motherhood."[3]

In this new era, women were encouraged to take a more active role in the shaping of their children's character; this was, after all, a new nation hoping to people itself with idealistic, patriotic, and moral citizens. As fathers became less involved in home life and more involved in the political activities of the developing nation, mothers, for the first time, were seen as performing an essential civic role as they brought up the next generation of Americans. Historians refer to this new role for women as "republican motherhood," which simply means that through motherhood, women became invested in the formation of the new republic. Women were to instill in their children, particularly their sons, all the values and moral fortitude necessary for growing the new nation.[4]

This calling fit right in with the relatively new thinking about child development that had come out of Europe and traveled to the new land with the more educated settlers. John Locke's philosophy of the human mind as a "tabula rasa" held that a child was essentially a blank slate upon which outside influences, such as parents, would create the child's character. Put all of this together—the fervor of a new nation, the idea that children were an essential part of the growth of this new nation, and the belief that a child's character could be formed by intentional teaching—and you've got a whole new role for mothers.

Something else was happening in these early days of American history that shaped the way we view motherhood even today: the social construct of mother love. In the early 1800s, maternal love became not just the bond between mother and child but a necessary civic commodity.

One source of motherly encouragement, *American Ladies Magazine,* put it this way: "What are the good works of women which she was created to perform? She was born to perpetuate the reign of all good and gentle affections in the world, and to diffuse through all society a spirit of love, of forbearance, of happiness."[5] In other words, a mother's task was to instill love in her children so they might bring that love into the world and counteract the dangers of selfishness and individuality that threatened to take over the tender new nation. Maternal love was not just for the benefit of a child but of the whole society. A mother's worth could be measured by how effectively she loved her children.

Because love was a fundamental part of a mother's parenting toolbox, it was essential that it be sharpened. The innate love between a mother and child wasn't enough. Mother love needed to be refined to its purest form to prevent any of the less worthy human emotions from bleeding through. The "tabula rasa" theory led the parenting experts of the day to promote the idea that a mother's emotions, as well as her words, made an impression on her children. Lewis says, "Because everything about her could leave an indelible mark, [a mother] had to make certain that everything about her was designed to create the right impressions. . . . In this sense, the real work of child rearing was to be focused upon the woman herself, as she tried to make herself a fit model for imitation."[6]

Since children were so easily influenced, mothers were instructed to guard their emotions carefully, so as not to show any thought or feeling they didn't want to pass on to their children. Anger, frustration, annoyance, impatience, these all had to be hidden to avoid passing them on to a child. Looking at the parenting literature from the 1830s, Lewis reports that, "The mother 'must always be dignified, calm, consistent with herself. . . . She must never be observed to betray a weakness, changeableness or vascillation [sic] of character . . . the mother must be at all times, agreeable, entertaining and tender.'"[7] Sound familiar?

Lewis goes on to say that mothers were instructed to "craft a maternal persona, a woman who was quintessentially feeling and self-effacing. She must eradicate almost entirely all

40

evidence of will and intention. . . . She must create the illusion that she had subdued all feeling, any interest in self, and all desire to exercise power. She might reveal only the scintilla of the crafted self that escaped her extraordinary efforts at self-suppression."[8]

This squelching of natural emotion was seen as a necessary sacrifice of motherhood—all Americans were expected to put their own selfishness aside and instead seek the common good of the republic. It would have made perfect sense for nineteenth-century women to see this call as their civic as well as maternal duty. And so the all-loving, self-sacrificing mother was born.

The Undermining of Mothers

By the latter part of the nineteenth century, another shift began to impact the way culture viewed mothers and therefore the way mothers viewed themselves. Around that time, science became involved in the daily lives of people; the automobile, the telephone, and the electric lightbulb all promised to make life easier. Science, then, became a respected field that people trusted to better their lives. This translated into a belief that doctors might have some expertise in child rearing that mothers would find valuable. However, in time, that advice has come to not only supplement the natural instincts of mothers but to supplant them. Over the course of the last one hundred years, the popular view of motherhood has shifted from something a woman is particularly suited for to something she cannot do without the help of outsiders.

Historian Rima Apple calls this trend "scientific motherhood." It is "the insistence that women require expert scientific and medical advice to raise their children healthfully."[9]

She says, "Increasingly women were told not just that they needed to learn from scientific and medical expertise but that they needed to follow the directions of experts. This aspect of the ideology presented women with a tension-laden contradiction: it made them responsible for the health and welfare of their families, but it denied them control over child rearing. In other words, women were both responsible for their families and incapable of that responsibility."[10]

This addition to the motherhood myth served to strip away the confidence women once had in their mothering abilities. While the women of early America saw themselves as performing an essential civic duty, their descendants were told that their efforts weren't enough, that if left to their own devices, mothers would ruin their children. In 1935, the editor of *Parents' Magazine* wrote, "Doctors, teachers, nutritionists and research workers are daily proving that not mother love alone but mother love in combination with the best that science has to offer in all fields of child care is needed."[11]

The reliance on science culminated in the 1946 release of Dr. Spock's *Baby and Child Care,* a tome read religiously by several generations of mothers. Spock's expertise was child psychology, and his book promoted the notion that a mother needed professional help not only with the physical aspects of child rearing but the emotional side as well. While the intent of the book was to empower women by encouraging them to rely on their own instincts, the results actually undercut the confidence of women who still felt the need to turn to a book to tell them they didn't need books.[12]

At the heart of most parenting guides is the message that mothers hold in their arms unformed humans who can be potentially damaged in countless ways. Pick them up when they cry and you'll spoil them. Let them cry and you'll inhibit their ability to trust. Feed them on a schedule or they'll learn to manipulate you. Feed them when they want to eat or you'll teach them not to listen to their bodies. Psychologist Eda LeShan once said, "If I were a young parent today I might cut my throat. . . . [R]aising a child today seems to have become about as pleasurable as trying to build a house without blueprints, and with faulty materials. The specter of its coming out crooked or falling apart is ever present."[13]

The result of all this advice has been a loss of confidence that women have not recovered in the one hundred years since the birth of scientific motherhood. You don't need to look any further than your local Barnes & Noble to see that the legacy of this reliance on experts is alive and well in American culture today. Over at the magazine rack, the cover of a recent issue of *Parenting* magazine lists the following stories: "Getting Your Child to Listen"; "'Is My Baby Eating Enough?'"; "How to Make Your Child Feel Loved"; and "Winter Safety Guide." The magazine world's other parenting heavy hitter, *Parents,* features "50 Best Snacks for Kids"; "Your Expert Guide to Good Behavior 24/7"; "20 Ways to Make Your Kids Feel Special"; and "30 Great Tips Your Busy Pediatrician Didn't Tell You." While there is nothing inherently wrong with these articles, they do promote the idea that mothers need experts to parent their children effectively.

Things don't get better in the parenting book section. Nearly every book on the shelf is designed to help women (there are a few specifically for fathers, but the majority are targeted at women) "fix" some aspect of their parenting—their child's behavior, diet, learning problem, social conflict, sleep issue, and so forth. Naturally, these books can be extremely helpful, but for the most part, this abundance of expert advice gives mothers the sense there is always a parenting crisis around the next bend that we are incapable of dealing with on our own. You may have gotten by so far, these books seem to say, but just you wait.

When my daughter was born, I was living ten hours away from my parents, I didn't have any friends who were at home with their children, and I hardly knew anyone with a baby. Much of what I learned about caring for my daughter I learned from books. They were particularly helpful when she wouldn't sleep, when she spit up after every meal, and when I worried that her never-ending cradle cap was the sign of some awful skin disorder.

To be honest though, I also found that most of the parenting books and articles I read actually made parenting harder. Before my daughter was born, I was flipping through one of my books, looking over a section about what to have in the "nursery" (that's in quotes because our nursery was the corner of the one bedroom in our apartment). After a few pages of reading about how far apart the crib slats should be so the baby's head wouldn't get stuck and how to choose a crib sheet that wouldn't pull off and strangle her, I had to stop. All I could think about was how many different ways there were for my baby to be killed or maimed simply because I chose the wrong bedding. All my reading made me a little more informed but a lot more paranoid.

And that's just the physical part of parenting. Even now, when I flip through a parenting magazine, I'm filled with a sense of incompetence. I feel as if I'm failing my children because I don't make carrot and raisin smiley faces on their peanut butter sandwiches (Is there enough fun in our family?). We don't do clever crafts together, and we don't have a special rainy day box of homemade puzzles (Am I providing enough creative outlets?). There is always some new report on why juice is bad for kids or how my daughter is more likely to be obese than a child born twenty years ago. More to the point, the overall message is that I can never do too much for my kids. I can never be too vigilant about keeping them safe. I can never rest in my quest to be a better mother because there is always more to learn.

Sure, some of this information is essential to our children's health. Having babies sleep on their backs has helped the SIDS rate drop by some 40 percent. Our children are better off for being in car seats and for not being exposed to lead paint. I firmly believe that parents need to be intentional about character formation and spiritual development. But sometimes all this helpful information can get to be too much. Our kids are safer and healthier, but we mothers are more confused, more overwhelmed, and more afraid that we'll somehow mess up.

Our contemporary evangelical view of motherhood incorporates major themes from our cultural past. We still hold to the idea that the mother is the primary font of moral development in her children, that how they turn out rests in large part with her ability to parent them effectively. We still hold to the idea that a mother's greatest influence comes not only through what she does but how she feels about motherhood. There is very little room for frustration, impatience, or anger in the model of a good mother. We still hold to the idea that our own instincts as mothers are insufficient and that we need the help of experts to parent our children well.

One thing that makes breaking through the myths of motherhood so difficult is that we have bought into them so wholeheartedly we have a hard time understanding motherhood in any other way. Even while I'm writing about this, part of me is thinking, *Yep, loving, patient, giving—that's all part of being a good mother.* But the other part of me has come to see that our definition of what makes a woman a "good" mother—the self-sacrifice, the morally righteous children, the veneer of placid tranquility—sets up a standard that is impossible for women to attain. As a result of these myths, we feel constantly defeated by our inability to measure up to the expectations of our culture.

Despite the fact that these expectations have lasted for centuries, my hunch is that they have always caused women to feel inadequate. In the nineteenth century, a "good" mother was one who kept her emotions hidden and passed nothing but good character on to her children. Now seriously, how many women do you think really pulled that off?

What makes this a relevant conversation for the church is that our Christian culture has adapted all this mythology as its own, turning what is essentially a secular understanding of motherhood into a Christian model. These expectations are stifling enough when they are promoted by our culture at large, but when religion is thrown into the mix, the result is crippling to the hearts of women. It's one thing to expect a mother to live up to this "good" mother model for the sake of her country; it's another to tie her work as a mother to her value as a child of God. And when the myths of motherhood—ideals that are impossible to live up to—take on the veneer of biblical truth, women suffer the devastating guilt of both ruining their children and failing their God.

Case Study

As I've talked to women about motherhood it has become clear to me that dashed expectations are the rule, not the exception. My friend Isabelle was 30 weeks pregnant with twins when one of them died. The birth of her first child was clouded with the grief of a second child lost. My friend Stacey married a man who quickly became abusive, leaving her with no choice but to take her daughter and escape to safety—a move that left her without a place to live and very little money to live on. I know women who have suffered multiple miscarriages and the stillbirth of their children; women who have tried everything possible to get pregnant with no result; women who have adopted children who nearly tore their new families apart; women whose husbands have become drug addicts, alcoholics, child molesters; women who struggle through their own addictions to painkillers or alcohol. These are Christian women who go to MOPS and the Tuesday morning Bible study in the Fellowship Hall. They are women who desperately want to live the lives they believe other mothers are living, but who feel themselves falling farther and farther away from the ideal life they once imagined for themselves.

Erica is one of these women. Her family has suffered from alcoholism, abuse, and just plain bad luck. And yet Erica says: "What we thought was the worst situation our family could face became our greatest blessing. We have truly experienced God's love and the joys of sharing this with one another. As a family, we have rediscovered the thrill of living and the gifts bestowed upon us each day, to embrace the beauty that is around us as well as within us all."

Erica found healing through trusted friends who opened their homes to her family. She saw God in the lives of other mothers who shared their own disappointments as well as their belief that God would always bring good out of bad. In the face of extraordinary disappointment and the loss of every ideal she ever had about motherhood and family life, Erica told me, "My life has definitely been different than I ever expected, harder and more challenging, but I have also learned more about who I am as a human being and a child of God then I ever could've imagined."

4

MOTHERING GOD'S WAY

When my daughter was about three, she went through a phase in which she didn't like to wear socks. To this day, I don't know what it was about socks that bothered her—I tried the kind with no toe seams, the kind *with* toe seams, tights, anklets, every kind of sock available—but for two months, she freaked out whenever she had to wear them. Unfortunately, those two months fell right in the middle of winter.

Most of the time, I could get her to put on a pair of pink or purple socks—the color seemed to override whatever comfort issues she had. But one morning, she just flat out refused to put on socks. It was about twenty degrees outside and there was snow on the ground, so I was rather insistent that she wear socks. In addition to the no-sock thing, she was also determined to wear her clogs. When I told her she needed to wear boots, she again refused.

After twenty minutes of going around and around about this, I had used all my best parenting tricks to get her to put on socks and boots to no avail (including holding her on her bed while I tried to put the socks on her, which, if you've ever tried putting socks on someone who doesn't want to wear socks, you know is a whole lot harder than it sounds). Finally, in exasperation, I said to her, "You're lucky you have a mother who doesn't spank!" and walked out of the room to get myself ready for work.[1]

I know some of you are thinking that a spanking is exactly what my daughter needed at that moment, that in letting her get away with disobedience, I gave up my God-given authority. And you might be right. It is entirely possible I was a lousy mother that morning. It wouldn't have been the first time, and it certainly won't be the last.

One of the more insidious results of the cult mentality in churches has been the way in which the false model of the "good" mother has been translated into expectations about *how* we parent. Remember Martha with the reflux baby? After weeks of struggling to nurse, she says, "Finally, I began bottle feeding. I felt so much relief and finally began to enjoy my baby. Still, I felt constant pressure from fellow Christians to explain why I wasn't nursing. I couldn't just say we gave up nursing. I had to qualify my decision by explaining my daughter's medical needs and even divulging my psychological struggle. If I didn't go into detail, my decision was not validated by other women."

Martha is not the only mother to feel as though she has to defend her parenting choices to other Christians. Some of the mothers I surveyed spoke of the pressure to circumcise (or not), to let their babies sleep with them (or not), to send their three-year-olds to preschool (or not). One woman told me that her friend had been nearly run out of church for not following the *Growing Kids God's Way* philosophy. Sadly, it is these outward expressions of parenting, not the spirit of a mother's relationship with her children, that many Christians use to measure what kind of mother a person is. And nothing exemplifies this attitude more than the conversations about spanking and homeschooling.

Sparing the Rod

I can't tell you how many casual conversations I've had with other mothers that come to an awkward standstill when we discover we don't have the same feelings about spanking. More than any other parenting issue, the question of spanking carries with it the full weight of a mother's theology. The evangelical take is typically: real Christians spank; liberal Christians don't.

The whole spanking issue centers on Proverbs 13:24, which says, "He who spares the rod hates his son, but he who loves him is careful to discipline him." I have a hunch that if Solomon, the king who wrote most of the book of Proverbs, had known what a fuss his words would cause in the kingdom he might have rephrased things. This is not the book for a long discussion of what that verse does or doesn't mean. There are Christian parenting experts on both sides of the issue, and they often use the same verses to make their case. I will tell you that we don't spank our children, and I am not a big fan of spanking as a discipline tool. At the same time, I have a few dear friends who spank and who have found it to be an effective method of discipline. I don't think ill of those friends, and I know them well enough to know that they have made their decision to spank with the same care and prayer we've put into our decision not to.

Still, many parents who spank feel ambivalent about

51

it. Anna is the mother of two young children. After being raised in a fairly conservative Christian home, she moved a little more to the left during her college years. Not long after becoming a mother, she heard a sermon at her parents' church on why parents should spank. She says, "I don't remember what else he said about discipline because I was so upset by the spanking remarks."

But Anna says things changed when her son turned two. "I had set up my tent in the 'no-spanking' camp and read up on all the ways to discipline while not resorting to violence. I tried all the different approaches, but they didn't work. I'd have him sit in the bathroom for his time-outs and sometimes he'd be in there for forty-five minutes before he'd calm down. He'd kick at the door or fling water around. Once he pulled the vanity away from the wall. So I've spanked him at times. I hate it, but it does tend to work. It seems to be a good deterrent when time-outs aren't cutting it or when the crime seems to warrant something more. But I've never been happy about it."

Anna's feelings about spanking are less surprising than her reluctance to open up about the issue with other Christian moms. She says, "I would never admit that I spank to my non-spanking friends, because who needs to hear their judgment? And I don't want to talk about it with my friends who spank because I don't want to get the 'I told you so' response. The bottom line is, every time I spank him and most of the time when I discipline him I feel like I'm failing at something that shouldn't be so difficult for me to do."

At the heart of the spanking debate is a set of assumptions about who we are to be as Christians. As mothers, we are supposed to know how to control our children, to discipline them into a state where they don't act out, don't misbehave, don't disobey. But this emphasis on the outward signs of good behavior fails to take into account the actual purpose of discipline, which is character formation.

In my reading about the issue, I have yet to find anyone who claims spanking contributes to character formation. Those who support spanking tend to talk about it in terms of obedience, of behavior. Roy Lessin, author of *Spanking, A Loving Discipline,* talks about spanking as an essential part of *training* a child, a word that implies behavior rather than motivation or character. And despite substantial evidence that children who are routinely spanked tend to be more violent and depressed as adults and actually respond with more, not less, antisocial behavior as children,[2] the Christian community still holds spanking up as "God's" way of discipline.

When an authority figure such as Roy Lessin tells parents that "spanking is an essential part of a parent's discipline toolbox,"[3] he's not leaving much room for disagreement. To think differently is to go against God. But there's nothing in the Bible, and certainly nothing in child development circles, to suggest that spanking is the only way to discipline a child. And yet so many Christians insist that it is.

It's worth looking at what the apostle Paul has to say about issues that divide the church. Paul can be a little hard to understand on some points, but he is extraordinarily clear on the issue of unity among Christians (Rom. 14:19; Eph. 4:3). Much of what Paul writes in his letters to various New Testament churches focuses on being less rule oriented and more love oriented. He advises the Jews not to worry about all the Gentiles being circumcised because such a demand causes more problems than it solves. In Romans, he says, "If your brother is distressed because of what you eat, you are no longer acting in love. . . . For the kingdom of God is not a matter of eating and drinking, but of righteousness, peace and joy in the Holy Spirit" (Rom. 14:15, 17).

The same could be said of spanking. Is it really worth arguing with our fellow Christians about? Is spanking so essential to godly parenting that we should let our support of other mothers die on that hill as it were? Not even close.

Holy Homeschooling

A couple of years ago, I made a decision to run an article in *Christian Parenting Today* that I expected would raise some eyebrows. It was called "I Was a Homeschool Dropout." The woman who wrote the piece chronicled her experience as a homeschooling parent and her decision to stop and send her children to public school instead.

The crux of the article was that this woman made her decision to homeschool based on what she thought was the "Christian" thing to do, despite her sense that it wasn't the right move for her family. When she stopped doing what she thought was expected and sought God's wisdom on the issue, she felt convicted that the better choice for her and her kids was for them to attend public school. Several years later, she firmly believes she made the right choice. Nowhere in the piece did she denigrate homeschooling. Nowhere did she suggest her story was anything other than her experience. Really, the article was less about homeschooling and more about paying attention to God's leading rather than to the pressures of Christian culture.

I fully expected to get mail about this article. About one-third of the *CPT* audience homeschools, so I knew the piece would hit a nerve. Sure enough, the emails came flooding in. But they weren't the letters I expected.

The vast majority of the response to the piece was incredibly positive. "Thank you, thank you, thank you!" wrote several women, grateful that they weren't alone in their experience of finding that homeschooling wasn't for them. Letter after letter rolled in thanking us for running an article that offered a point of view on homeschooling not often found in Christian literature.

Many of these readers had never shared their stories with other Christians because they felt judged for having "failed" at homeschooling. One mother wrote, "Talk about timing! I just recently shed my last waterfall of tears about the decision not to homeschool my children. Like the author of the article, I too had visions of a happy, harmonious, holy homeschooling family. But it seemed the more I held on to that plan, the more stressed and without joy I became." Over and over, these women had been given the impression that they had not only failed as homeschoolers but as Christian mothers as well. They were incredibly grateful to discover that maybe they weren't terrible mothers after all.

Along with all the glowing letters came a batch of angry responses. What surprised me was not what these readers thought—as I said, I expected some of them to be bothered—but how mean-spirited they were in their opinions. One reader wrote, "What a shame [the author] allowed her unruly son, apathetic husband, discouraging friends and neighbors, and her own skittish personality to open up her ears to Satan's whispers that she mistakenly took to be the voice of God." She went on to denigrate public schools as unbiblical and under the control of Satan. Not exactly a helpful reaction to someone struggling with a difficult decision.

Many other negative letters blamed the author's lack of character, discipline, you name it, for her decision to stop homeschooling, as though her personal failings were the only explanation for why homeschooling didn't work for her family. These readers didn't think it was possible for the author to have come to a conclusion about homeschooling that was different from theirs and still be inside of God's will.

Here again, I'm not going to spend time debating the merits of homeschooling or public school or private school. I only wish to point out that there is tremendous pressure to parent a certain way, pressure that is not based in Scripture.

As far as I can tell, the opinion of the angry woman above is not the view of the Christian homeschooling establishment. In fact, most of the legitimate resources for homeschoolers take exactly the opposite approach, making it very clear that homeschooling might not be for everyone. Michael Farris, founder of the Home School Legal Defense Association and one of the biggest national advocates of Christian home-schooling, writes, "Even though I think that homeschooling is the greatest form of education, and that any parents can do a great job of homeschooling if they are willing to work hard, and even though I think Scripture teaches me as a Christian father that this is my obligation to my children, I refuse to tell anyone else that it is a sin for them to fail at homeschool. There is only one Holy Spirit, and He 'ain't' me. And He 'ain't' you either."[4]

Farris notes that what he calls the "homier than thou" attitude exists within the homeschool community as well—a kind of "spiritual one-upmanship."[5] My friend Ellen just started homeschooling one of her three sons. She says she has been told that she's not *really* homeschooling because she's using a tutoring program rather than one of the "preferred" curriculums. Here she is, taking a chance on this pretty radi-cal way of living and she's not even finding support from within the homeschool community.

Sharon is the mother of three biological children and has also cared for more than twenty-five foster children. She told me, "I presently homeschool our foster children, but our other children attended public school. We were looked down upon for 'throwing our children to the wolves.' But my kids stood up for their beliefs, led Bible studies, gave hope in the middle of crisis (we lived in Colorado during the school shootings at Columbine), and stopped at least three abortions by counseling their friends."

The passage that many homeschoolers cite in their commitment to homeschooling is Deuteronomy 6:7, which tells parents to teach children to love God "when you sit at home and when you walk along the road, when you lie down and when you get up." While I think it's perfectly fine to read that passage as justification for teaching children at home, I disagree that it requires parents to do so, primarily because this verse isn't talking about school or even the Ten Commandments.

According to biblical scholars, this verse is really a secondary point in Moses' main message. The real heart of Moses' words to the Israelites comes in Deuteronomy 6:4–5 where Moses tells the people, "The LORD our God, the LORD is one. Love the LORD your God with all your heart and with all your soul and with all your strength." *This* is what we are to teach our children and bind on our foreheads and write on our doorframes. Moses uses hyperbole to make his point: that we are to take this call seriously. It is the *content* of what we teach our children that concerns Moses, not the method.

Throughout Deuteronomy, God is calling the people of Israel to a new kind of life, a life where they consider others, where they put away their superstitious belief in false idols and instead live by faith in God. God's commands all center on living a life that moves away from the pagan culture and honors God. Moses understood that doing so was going to take a lot of work and a lot of teaching—centuries worth in fact.

In our day, that can certainly include homeschooling our kids, but I don't think it's limited to such a decision. God commands us to be intentional in teaching our children to love God and to live our faith consistently. The goal is for God to be so entrenched in our families that our children know our lives are guided by faith. There is no sense in this passage—or anywhere else in the Bible—that there is only one way to do these things.

It's worth noting that the homeschool movement has really built up steam during a period when public school test scores have gotten worse, violence in schools has increased, and some districts have developed more "liberal" curriculums in areas such as sex education. It seems pretty clear that the increase in homeschooling has more to do with the state of our schools and less with some long-standing evangelical emphasis on home education. (Until the creation of public education as we know it in the mid-1800s, no one was educated in the formal sense at all.) If the Bible has always commanded parents to homeschool, why haven't we been doing it all along? It's a fair question to ask as we look at the ways culture has infiltrated the church's view of motherhood. The desire to keep our children safe, to have more control over what they're learning, to guard their innocence a little longer—these are all perfectly reasonable motivations for educating children at home. But to suggest that the Bible commands parents to homeschool is just plain wrong.

The voice of the homeschooling community has been incredibly effective in gaining legitimacy for this form of education, but it's unfortunate some edges of that voice have led mothers to feel that they don't have the same access to God's leading as these families. When the message is that homeschooling (or private school or public school) is the *only* choice for Christian parents, we deny that God can and does lead us all down different paths. We deny that children are unique and need to be treated as such. We deny that what works for one family really might not work for another.

Cookie-Cutter Parenting

These issues point to a larger assumption about parenting, namely that all Christians ought to live under the same set of family values promoted by the evangelical community. In fact, I've always thought that until the rise of the evangelical movement, Christians didn't put a whole lot of thought into family values. I've also always thought that evangelicals were responsible for influencing the secular culture's conversation about family and bringing the family into the political realm.

Wrong. It turns out that secular culture and mainline Protestants actually led the way on family issues long before evangelicals entered the fray. Historian Margaret Lamberts Bendroth says, "The family was the province of more theologically liberal Protestants for most of the twentieth century; even sexuality issues associated with the family—abortion, homosexuality, and premarital and extramarital sex—alarmed mainline Protestants far earlier than they did fundamentalists and conservative evangelicals. . . . The pro-family movement emerged when religious conservatives were beginning to feel a sense of cultural power in the wake of Southern Baptist Jimmy Carter's presidential election. . . . By the early 1970s, evangelicals had constructed a media empire around the family and related issues of gender roles, child discipline, and the moral hazards of adultery and divorce."[6] In other words, evangelicals jumped on a bandwagon; they had very little to do with building it. They saw an opportunity for influence and grabbed it.

And so arose the legions of evangelical parenting experts who fill the shelves of Christian bookstores. Like Dr. Spock in the '50s, these experts have become the voice of reason, guidance, and comfort for thousands of overwhelmed Christian parents. What gives them special resonance with Christians is the inclusion of spiritual advice along with the tips on getting babies to sleep and eat, getting toddlers to obey, and getting teenagers to listen. But much like the shift from maternal instinct to expert advice that came along with the rise of scientific motherhood, the influx of Christian parenting experts has led Christian mothers to stifle their own instincts and instead follow the generic prescriptions of others.

I believe we parents need all the help we can get in raising our children. I also firmly believe that it's a very, very good thing for the church to help parents see the importance of being purposeful in nurturing the spiritual development of our children. Where the "expert" issue becomes problematic for me, and for so many mothers, is when the church suggests that (1) we should all be listening to the same experts, and (2) the opinions of Christian experts are more valid than our own instincts. The result is that we feel incapable of parenting our children, we feel incompetent because we can't possibly do everything these experts suggest, and we feel guilty for failing to be the parents the experts tell us to be. Most of all, we get the distinct impression that we put our children in spiritual danger if we slip up. Such a message is inconsistent with God's promise that we are saved by the blood of Christ and not through human action.

And so we spank because Roy Lessin says we should

or we homeschool because all the other Christian moms we know tell us it's a good idea. Such specific demands on godly mothers point to a deeper theology in the evangelical community. These discussions are less about discipline or education or parenting theories than they are about control. For some reason, the church has made controlling our children, molding them to fit a certain slot, the primary goal of Christian parenting. My friend Cecilia calls it "cookie-cutter parenting."

The job of the church is to help us figure out how to live as God's people in every aspect of our lives, including our parenting. But too often, the church is less concerned with the process of formation (both in adults and children) and more concerned about obedience and outward expressions of propriety and faith. Hence the emphasis on well-behaved children.

The pressure to parent a certain way is the logical outgrowth of a brand of thinking that is not unique to evangelicals. Whenever you have a group of people who meet together for an expressed purpose, that group will tend to define itself with certain expectations about the way members of that group think and act. Indeed, the evangelical community is notorious for having a who's in, who's out mentality. Bendroth notes, "Well before the Christian Coalition emerged in the national media, a dedicated group of neoevangelical leaders discovered that family matters resonated with churchgoers, providing clear lines between the godly and the unrighteous. Such issues allowed preachers to invoke personal and social morality; and they laid down moral boundaries that differentiated believers from nonbelievers."[7]

The criteria set out by evangelicals for being a good Christian parent find their roots in a lot of places but not

THE MYTH OF THE PERFECT MOTHER

in the Bible. While the Bible ought to guide our parenting, it's a mistake to think that it tells us how to parent. The Bible tells us how to follow God (something we ought to do in every part of our lives, including our relationships with our children). It tells us what God has done and will continue to do for us and how God's followers have responded to God throughout history. It tells us how to live as God's people—whether we are parents or not. It's just plain spiritual malpractice to suggest that the Bible offers specific instructions on how we are to discipline or educate or otherwise relate to our children.

I am a woman of faith who doesn't spank. I am a Christian mother who will likely never homeschool. Are these dictums on how we are to parent really part of the call of the gospel? Am I really failing as a Christian mother because my daughter goes to time-out rather than across my knee? Is my immortal soul in jeopardy because my child goes to public school? Is hers? Is my child's relationship with God so tenuous that it is dependent on my human frailty to survive? I didn't think so.

A Case Study

My friend Barbara is the mother of eleven kids. She is a committed Christian and a devoted homeschooler, but she also recognizes that each of her children has different educational needs and that those needs can change from year to year. So some of her kids have only been homeschooled; others have done a mix of homeschool and public school; still others have done some private school, some public, and just a touch of homeschooling. What I love about Barbara's approach is that she looks at the needs of her children and figures out what's going to work best for each child—not just educationally but emotionally, socially, and spiritually as well. She hasn't let ideology get in the way of letting God lead her as a mother.

Decisions about how to discipline our children and what kind of schooling they need ought to come from our understanding of who our children are, not who we think they should be. We would do well to read up on learning styles, multiple intelligence, and personalities to shore up our belief that God creates every child with a unique set of gifts and talents and ways of understanding the world.

If you haven't assessed your personality or learning style, try it. Plenty of websites and books offer short tests that can provide incredible insight into your way of thinking as well as the mind-set of your children. During a work retreat, our *CPT* staff took a short version of the Myers-Briggs personality inventory. When we realized that one of our editors processed information in a completely different way than the rest of us, we were able to communicate on a much more effective level.

For parents, it's always tempting to assume our children think like we do, but the truth is, they don't, at least not all the time. I have often heard Emily ask Jimmy a question and listened as he answers her in a way I know won't make sense to her because she thinks more like me than like him. The same communication hurdles we have in our marriage pop up in Jimmy's relationship with Emily.

When it comes to discipline and schooling, we owe it to our children to know them, to understand what makes them act and think the way they do, and to adjust our expectations and ways of nurturing them accordingly.

5

THE TRUTH ABOUT DEPRESSION

The weight of the intense expectations placed on Christian mothers can lead to all kinds of emotional and spiritual struggles. Perhaps the most misunderstood—and least talked about—by-product of motherhood is depression.

When you think about depression, you probably think of the debilitating, keep-the-shades-closed-and-stay-in-bed-all-day kind of intense sadness that sends people to the edge of suicide, if not past it. But depression is actually much more common, and much more varied, than most of us realize. Many people suffer from what I call "high-functioning" depression, which is similar to high-functioning alcoholism. These people might look perfectly fine on the outside, but there are serious problems within. I am one of them.

For several years, I haven't felt quite right. I used to be a confident, outgoing, fun-loving gal, but as I moved into my late twenties, I began to get exhausted by people, I lost confidence in my ability to develop friendships, and I had no idea what I wanted to do with my life. I attributed these feelings to not having a fulfilling job, or living too far away from friends and family, or needing some time to myself.

Yet even after I found a fantastic job, moved to a wonderful neighborhood in the same state as my parents and many dear friends, and made more time for solitude, I still felt this lingering dullness in my life, as if I was living in a haze that kept me from feeling connected to the world. While researching this book, I came to believe I was suffering from a long-term bout of depression. I saw a psychologist who confirmed my self-diagnosis. I now go to biweekly counseling with a Christian therapist and take an antidepressant every day. I still have work to do, but I can tell I'm feeling a whole lot better.

I'm not getting all confessional on you so you'll feel sorry for me.[1] Rather, I'm letting you in on my big secret because I think my experience reflects that of a great many women. If you met me, you'd never guess I'm depressed. I smile. I laugh. I get out of bed every morning to care for my children. My house is reasonably clean. While today I happen to look like an unkempt mom complete with sweatshirt and ponytail, most days I try to put a little effort into my appearance or at least wear pants that don't involve elastic. I don't sit around crying in my darkened room or leave my children unattended while I sleep away the afternoon. Even my husband has had a hard time believing I'm depressed because I don't fit the typical image of a depressed person.

Still, as I read about depression, I recognized that much of what I was feeling was completely in line with its symptoms. I was easily irritated and overwhelmed; I didn't sleep well; I never felt like eating (although I did); I had very little energy and zero interest in sex. I had a hard time making real connections with people because I was so out of touch with my inner world that I couldn't form opinions on even the most banal subject. It took too much energy to call people or make plans, and I usually turned down social situations because they seemed like too much effort. I was cut off from my emotions to the point that I couldn't even figure out a truthful answer to someone's "How are you?" I rarely felt great joy or great sorrow—just a disinterest in the world around me. Despite all of this, and despite knowing quite a bit about depression, it never occurred to me that I was experiencing anything other than a normal reaction to life as a busy, tired woman.

There are lots of moms just like me who go through their days with the veneer of having their act together while inside they know they are barely managing to get through till bedtime. Sadly, many of these women don't realize that the numbness they feel might be indicative of a real illness that will only get worse if left untreated. In their excellent book *Unveiling Depression in Women,* Dr. Archibald Hart, Dean Emeritus of the Graduate School of Psychology at Fuller Theological Seminary, and his daughter, Christian psychotherapist Catherine Hart Weber, note that, "Mothers have to deal with a constant flow of pressures and the 'chronic strain of the mundane,' everyday home management, baby nurturing, and toddler parenting, not to mention the care of teenagers and husbands. . . . These demands are all part of modern life, and they don't necessarily lead to clinical depression. That doesn't mean we should underestimate their effects. The cumulative outcome of trying to survive while keeping up with the rest of the human race, with no opportunity for respite, can lead to a devastating depression."[2]

Sadder still, most of these women will never talk about their feelings with fellow Christians simply because there is so much shame attached to being less-than-thrilled with our lives as mothers. Many women have a hard time admitting these feelings even to themselves. During a casual phone conversation with a friend of mine who lives in another state, my friend hinted at her own struggle with depression, one that followed much the same path as my own. Amazingly, we had spent time together and talked about everything else during the several years we lived in the same area, but we never even came close to revealing that we were dealing with these feelings—honestly, I don't think either of us knew we were depressed at the time. What a tragedy that our pride, shame, and ignorance kept us from digging into these experiences together.

Depression and Motherhood

Even if you're not experiencing some form of depression, the odds are very good that a woman you know is. Recent studies have suggested that some 21 percent of women in America have experienced at least one major depressive episode in their lives. That means it's likely that one of every five women you know has been or will become depressed.[3] Other studies show that women are two to three times more likely than men to report signs of depression. According to Hart and Weber, depression is one of the most significant health risks for women of childbearing and child-rearing age.[4] Rather than be surprised when a mother becomes depressed, we should be shocked that there aren't more of us openly talking about what is a remarkably common experience.

There are times in a woman's life when feelings of depression are the natural response to a life-altering situation. Most women experience a mild depression a few weeks after giving birth, and some go into a deeper postpartum depression. (Less common but much more dangerous is postpartum psychosis, which is what some experts believe caused Andrea Yates's breakdown.) Depression is also a necessary part of the grieving process that comes after a loss, such as the death of a parent or a move away from friends.

Typically, these forms of depression don't throw us because we have a sense of why we feel the way we do and we believe there will be an end to this period of deep sadness. And yet one of the reasons I was unaware of my depression is because I always found an explanation for why I felt the way I did: not enough sleep, too much stress at work, no intimate friendships, wrong house, wrong town, wrong body, whatever. However, the DSM-IV,[5] the standard diagnostic tool of mental health professionals, doesn't define depression by its cause but by its severity. Getting to the "why" behind a depression is really the second step in dealing with it. The first step is to acknowledge that the symptoms are real and that help is needed.

As I mentioned, most of us think we know what depression looks like, but there are many symptoms we experience without tripping on the idea that they could be related to depression. Hart and Weber note that "depression is considered 'clinical' when symptoms are severe and include difficulty getting through a daily routine, sleeping too much or too little, disturbance of concentration, excessive negativity or pessimistic thoughts, severe guilt, and an inability to connect with or be around others. . . . Depression can make you feel overwhelmed, anxious, worthless, and hopeless, and you might even have thoughts about ending your life."[6] Women in particular also experience atypical symptoms, such as oversleeping, increased appetite and resultant weight gain, anxiety, guilt over not getting things accomplished, sensitivity to rejection, and self-consciousness.[7] When I first read this description, I was struck by the idea that much of what mothers experience each day—exhaustion, anxiety, guilt, a sense of failure, the feeling of not really connecting with people—can be aspects of depression.

What was equally striking was how common these feelings are in the Christian women I surveyed. In my questionnaire, I included a list of statements and asked the women to check those that indicated an experience they'd had as a mom. Here are a few of them:

- Sometimes I feel really angry toward my children.
- There are days when I have a hard time getting out of bed even though I've had a full night's sleep.
- I often feel really lonely.
- I worry a lot that my children will get into trouble one day, even though I've tried to raise them with good values.
- Some days I don't like being a mother.
- I have a lot of fear that something bad will happen to my children.
- I struggle with feelings of guilt about the way I parent.
- I have had moments where I've imagined hurting or leaving my children.

The majority of the women checked at least three of these, with anger, loneliness, and guilt being the most common experiences. That these women have experienced symptoms of depression doesn't necessarily mean they are depressed, but it does show that many Christian mothers struggle with feelings that could lead to depression if they aren't dealt with in an honest, compassionate environment.

These feelings can come from one of two places—Hart and Weber differentiate between biological-based and situational-based depressions. As you can guess, biological depression means the brain's chemistry is off. Situational depression (also called reactive depression) is brought on by something outside of ourselves. Both are valid, real forms of depression and sometimes both causes are at fault. For this discussion, I'm going to focus on the situational-based depression, because it's clear to me that depression in mothers often grows out of the clash between their hopes for themselves as mothers (hopes often formed through the cult-of-the-family mentality found in evangelical circles) and the reality of what mothering is really like.

Living the Dream

Think back to when you were a child. When you imagined your life as an adult, it probably didn't include driving the minivan to swim practice at 5:00 in the morning or being bone tired from a day of keeping up with two kids under four. You probably didn't envision yourself mopping the kitchen floor twice a day or scrambling to get three kids ready for school while you took a two-minute shower before heading to your boring job. You likely never imagined there would be days when you didn't like your children or would lack the patience to answer their never-ending questions.

For nearly every mother I surveyed, motherhood has proven much more demanding than they thought. Candace, the mother of five, said, "I dreamed of having the perfect family and becoming my children's best friend. My expectations were that I would be a homeroom mom and do all these wonderful things for my children and everything would be wonderful. But I had no idea what sleepless nights and concern for their lives really meant. Your children don't just come out well behaved. I was not nearly as loving as I thought I would be. My children have irritated me and there have been times I wished they would go away." Candace is one of many moms who have discovered that their dreams of motherhood and their reality are not even close to being the same thing.

Aubrey, the mother of two, grew up believing that "good Christian mothers want to have children right away and must give up their careers. I felt that I should embrace motherhood with vigor and excitement. I thought that as a new mother I would be patient, kind, and able to maintain a household while having perfect children." In reality, she says, "I thought something was really, really wrong with me because I was suffering from depression after my son was born as well as tremendous anxiety about everything we were going through. I was unable to live up to the expectations that I could handle it all. Sometimes I just wanted to get away."

As a young girl I didn't dream of being a mother (I was pretty focused on figuring out how I would balance being a movie star *and* a backup singer with the Carpenters), but when I got married, I began to genuinely like the idea of having children. I pictured myself as the fun mom who was firm but silly, the one all the other kids liked to hang out with because I treated them with love and respect and really understood them. Now and then, I have days like that. But most days I'm lucky to get from breakfast to bedtime without feeling like a frazzled failure. Nearly every day, I have the sense that I haven't lived up to my own expectations, much less those of the church.

When a dream fades and a lesser reality takes its place, we experience loss. Yes, it's the loss of something that was never real, but the emotions involved in grieving a lost dream, a lost image of ourselves, are not unlike the emotions that come when we mourn a lost loved one. That's because our ideas of who we will be as mothers go to the heart of who we are as women. When we picture ourselves as mothers, we picture ourselves at our best, as the women we want to be, the mothers we believe we can be. When that dream is dashed and we come face-to-face with our own failings, we find it difficult to adapt to this diminished version of ourselves. We face the loss not just of a dream but of a chunk of our self-esteem that tells us we will rise to the incredibly important task of raising children. That loss becomes more acute when we see other women who seem to pull off motherhood with aplomb (she can do it so there must be something wrong with me), or when we run headlong into that false model of the "good" Christian mother (I'm not only a lousy mom, I'm a lousy Christian).

Kate is a lifelong Christian and the mom of three. She says, "Sometimes my faith causes me more guilt than if God were not on the throne of my life. I think I 'should' myself far too much, and I flub up all the time. I expected to be more patient and more fun to be with as a mom. I don't enjoy motherhood as much as I thought I would, and things don't seem to come as easily as they do for others I know who have the patience of saints and kids who are angels (at least from my observation!)."

When a woman feels as if she's failing her children because she's not the patient, creative, all-loving mother she wanted to be, the sense of loss will grow deeper. When she doesn't like her children, when she thinks about running away, when she's told her desire to work outside the home or stay home with her kids or take time for herself or pursue an interest outside of motherhood is selfish, that sense of loss will grow deeper still. Eventually, the depth of this loss can cause a woman to spiral into a serious depression.

Shiny Happy Mommies

Depression can also develop when a woman habitually keeps her emotions in check. Much of the mythology of motherhood has to do with the visage we present to the world. It involves not just what we do as parents but how we feel about motherhood as well.

There is a long history of feminist literature on how women have been socialized to be "good girls" who never get angry, never complain, never question authority. By now, we're all pretty well aware that this is a dangerous mold to squeeze into, and yet many of us, myself included, still work very hard to be good. So much of the depression women experience involves the emotional side of motherhood—we thought we'd like it more, we thought we'd be more patient, we didn't know we were capable of such intense anger and frustration. At the end of the day, we simply don't know how to deal with these emotions.

I grew up in Minnesota, land of stoic Scandinavian Lutherans, where emotions are not so much frowned upon as ignored. Nobility is defined by a person's ability to weather the good and the bad with equal temerity. Crying is a weakness, but so is enjoying yourself too much. As author Howard Mohr says, Minnesotans exaggerate in reverse: "Say, that's not too bad," is a supreme compliment. Yeah, it makes for funny jokes, but also emotionally vacant people.[8]

Because I grew up in a culture that doesn't provide much instruction about emotional intelligence, I have learned how to keep my feelings close to the vest. As a result, I've gotten to the point where I truly can't tell what I feel most of the time. Naturally, I felt tremendous joy when my children were born, but it was my husband who wept for half an hour at the miracle of our daughter, while I merely shed a few tears when telling my mom she was a grandmother. I am so detached from my emotions that I don't feel much genuine anger or genuine delight. Thankfully, that's changing as I work through my depression.

The church traditionally has offered little help when it comes to developing a healthy emotional life, especially when it comes to the so-called "negative" feelings: anger, fear, doubt, disappointment, sadness, frustration, anxiety, loneliness, and on and on. Back in the third chapter, I talked about the social construct of "mother love," the idea that a mother's love was so essential to the proper development of a child that a woman should never let her child see any other expression of emotion. One nineteenth-century parenting expert named John Abbott wrote, "We must bring our own feelings and our own actions under a rigid system of discipline, or it will be in vain for us to hope to curb the passions and restrain the conduct of those who are looking to us for instruction and example."[9] Unfortunately, that same message lives on in many evangelical churches.

Traci, the mother of three, says, "Many women in the church portray motherhood as Utopia, which it isn't. I have found it difficult to discuss the more trying aspects of being a mom with my church friends for fear of sounding like someone who shouldn't be a mother." As a result of the myth of the good Christian mother, women learn that their feelings of dissatisfaction, sadness, and anxiety are abnormal and need to be tucked away so they can put on their happy Christian mom faces. After a while, a woman's emotional life becomes bifurcated in such a way that she may not be able to even identify those feelings she's learned to ignore. The void left by those buried emotions is then filled with the kind of numbness and emotional disconnect that typifies depression.

Depression and the Church

There's a sad irony to this idea that the myth of the perfect Christian mother contributes to depression in women while at the same time the church is typically reluctant to acknowledge and deal with that depression. I know several depressed women who took the risk of talking to their pastor or a church friend about their feelings only to be told to pray harder, get their spiritual lives in order, or recognize that this season of life is all about self-sacrifice so they might as well get used to it. Rare is the voice that says, "A lot of mothers feel the way you do from time to time. If you can't shake these feelings in a couple of weeks, please let me help you find a way to work through them."

The overall message from the church is that we need to be grateful for the lives we have, that we need to find joy in all circumstances. That's a beautiful, biblically based message. The idea that God is at work even in difficult, painful situations is certainly one of the most comforting promises in God's Word. But we haven't made much room in the Christian life for dealing with the real pain people experience, particularly emotional pain.

In her wonderful book, *Holding on to Hope*, Nancy Guthrie[10] writes extensively about the ways in which the church has failed to give us tools for handling the suffering we will all experience in life. Instead of expecting suffering and learning to seek God in its midst—something that the Bible shows time and time again—we have been taught to pray it away, to beg for a cure or a solution or an end to our pain, as though it is somehow an anomaly in the Christian life.

I believe that the church tends to deal with depression—especially in mothers—in a similar way. To treat it as a wholly spiritual issue, one that can be healed by a deeper relationship with God, only addresses a piece of the depression puzzle. Depression is not primarily a state of mind or spirit but an actual illness with physical, emotional, and spiritual ramifications. Naturally prayer and a deeper relationship with God are invaluable in dealing with depression—a large part of my therapy involves my learning how to embrace the person God created me to be rather than trying to create some persona that people might like better. But to send the message that depression is basically the result of a spiritual failure is simply ignorant.

It's just as dangerous to treat depression in women as a failure on their part to embrace the joys of motherhood or to find completion in their role as homemaker. We all agree that God created us as unique people with individual gifts, interests, and perspectives on life. And yet we hold to this idea that every woman should respond to motherhood—one of the biggest upheavals she'll experience in life—with the same delight and passion.

It's interesting to me that one element of being a "good" mother is to nurture the God-given gifts in our children and see them as individuals for whom God has a unique purpose, while at the same time expecting women to fit into one specific mold of mothering. When we dismiss a woman's unhappiness with a role that she is not allowed to tailor to her own gifts, we essentially send the message that the person God created her to be, the life she senses God leading her toward, is somehow flawed. Talk about depressing.

A Case Study

In 2002, I had the good fortune to be part of the MOPS (Mothers of Preschoolers) International regional events.[11] These two-day affairs (there were four in all) involved a Friday night "girl time" of music and short talks, and a Saturday docket of seminars for MOPS leaders. I was part of the Friday night program along with Lisa Johnson and Carol Kuykendall.

One of my roles was to interview a pre-selected MOPS mom and find out how MOPS had impacted her life. I was surprised to find that three of the four women I talked to had struggled with a deep depression that had led them to consider suicide. For one woman, the depression was sparked by a stillbirth, for another, a series of miscarriages, and for the third, a move far away from family and friends. Each of them found help because of MOPS.

Those conversations were part of what got me thinking about writing this book. These women were chosen to speak because someone thought their stories would resonate with others. That meant they weren't alone in their experiences with depression, loneliness, and sadness. It also meant they had come through a terrible situation and moved to a place of spiritual and emotional well-being in part because of the care and concern of other moms.

As an organization, MOPS is very good at promoting itself as a ministry to moms with young children. Because of that, it's easy to dismiss them as one more place for stay-at-home moms to meet, have a snack, and learn some new crafting tip. But the stories I heard from these three women, as well as scores of others I heard at the events, have proven to me that something deeper is happening in these groups of women, something that has profoundly affected them. I left each weekend event craving the kind of supportive, caring, intimate friendships these women were experiencing.

Personally, I've always resisted "mom" groups. Maybe it's because I think about parenting for a living and have very little desire to spend my free time chatting about potty training and who's got new teeth. At the same time, I have been desperately lonely for years, searching fruitlessly for the kinds of friendships I had in college and graduate school—the kind where you know each other's deepest desires and dreams, where you form your understanding of yourself as you talk late into the night about God, poverty, romance, injustice, faith, philosophy. Honestly, I would have settled for someone who laughed at my jokes and was still willing to let me cry in front of them.

Back to my point. I've come to see that, like any group, MOPS groups are only as meaningful as moms allow them to be. It's easy to go into our default happy-mom mode when we gather with a group of mothers, but imagine how much more fulfilling and renewing our relationships could be if we let our pride slide away to reveal our real struggles and sorrows. Imagine where those three women would have ended up if they had lived out the myth of the Christian mom rather than making themselves vulnerable by laying out their real emotional states. Each one of them told of the incredible support they received from their MOPS friends once they took the chance of being vulnerable. Perhaps they experienced some judgment along the way, but ultimately, it was the Christlike compassion lived out in the lives of other mothers that saved them.

The idea that genuine, intimate friendships are an essential part of our emotional health is born out by a study from UCLA which suggests that when women are stressed, we release the hormone oxytocin, which encourages us to gather with other women. When we engage in tending our relationships, more oxytocin is released, which has a calming, stress-reducing effect. And get this: The Nurses' Health Study from Harvard Medical School suggests that not having close friends is actually detrimental to a woman's health.

MOPS is a wonderful organization, but it's certainly not the only means by which mothers can connect. Another woman told me that her church has a mothers' fellowship group that was her saving grace as a struggling mom. I've found a great deal of support and strength through my friendships with a few other women who have suffered from depression—some are mothers, some aren't. But no group of friends can do much of anything for us without our willingness to cut through the myth of the got-it-together mom and dig into the real emotional trials and triumphs of motherhood.

We moms can also improve our mental and spiritual health, not to mention the world around us, by taking off our motherhood blinders and finding ways to use our gifts outside of our families. Tremendous healing takes place when we shift our focus from our own lives to the lives of others. My friend Rosalyn is currently separated from her emotionally abusive husband and is living with her seven-year-old son in a friend's spare room. Her mother is cycling through a series of health problems that land her in the hospital at least once a month. Rosalyn is deeply in debt, struggling to balance work with single parenthood, suffering from her own physical and emotional issues, and trying to get the right kind of help for her son who has a slight learning disability. She hates the idea that she's nearly forty and is having to start her life all over again. She feels useless, depressed, and needy. Needless to say, she is beyond stressed out.

Recently, a friend from church asked if Rosalyn and her

son would be willing to spend an evening babysitting the three children of a single mother the church was trying to assist. Rosalyn certainly had every reason to say no, not the least of which was her concern that her son would be exposed to kids who use foul language, who have serious behavior issues, and who live in a dangerous neighborhood. But Rosalyn agreed to watch the kids, and she and her son spent several hours in a hot, cramped apartment trying to maintain some order with the three challenging children. When she was through, Rosalyn told me she felt that her own problems paled in comparison to those she had just experienced. She felt a new sense of gratitude for having a place to live, a steady job, and the support of good friends. More importantly, she felt good being the one with something to give. This experience didn't make Rosalyn's stress vanish, but in offering help to someone else, she knew that she still had gifts God could use to bless the world.

6

THE SOCIAL DISCONNECT

It happens all the time. My husband will come home from work and say, "Did you hear what happened?" Inevitably, he'll tell me about some news event that has everyone "out there" talking, while "in here" we're caught up in who had the purple silly straw first and why her brother should never be allowed to touch it again. It was noon on September 11, 2001, before I had any clue that something horrible had taken place a few hours earlier. When the towers fell, I was watching *Sesame Street* with my four-year-old. The world was literally crumbling, and I was oblivious.

That might not bother some people, but knowing what's going on in the world is a big deal to me. I like to talk about politics and literature and movies and music. I like knowing the latest news. I'm a huge celebrity gossip freak—give me a copy of *In Style* magazine and I'm on cloud nine. I'm the girl you want on your Trivial Pursuit team.

Back when I worked in the office every day, I had time to read the newspaper in the morning. I flipped through stacks of other magazines to stay in touch with popular culture. Whenever I went online, Yahoo News popped up and gave me an update on the day's events. I was the one coming home saying, "Did you hear what happened?" Because I work at the company that publishes *Christianity Today* magazine, I had a deeper awareness of the struggles of missionaries in war-torn nations and the political ramifications of George Bush's faith. I felt connected to the bigger world.

Then I started working at home. I hardly have time to tie my shoes much less read a paper. I may catch five minutes of Peter Jennings, but I usually can't hear him because there's a two-year-old in the room playing his drums. I'm not all that bothered by the lack of information coming into my head until I'm with other adults who say things like, "Can you believe this legislation that's going through?" or "Did you hear that Brad Pitt was in town yesterday looking for a thirty-seven-year-old mother to star in his next movie?"

We moms often joke that we have no idea what's going on in the "real world" because we haven't read a newspaper or stayed awake for an entire newscast since our children arrived. We laugh at how out of touch we are and move on to talking about what we do know—whose turn it is to drive to gymnastics, how to use a rectal thermometer, that kind of thing. But this sense of being dislodged from the world extends far beyond not knowing the latest news or trivia. Motherhood, particularly the brand of motherhood expected of Christian mothers, brings with it a kind of social disconnect that has a deep impact on the emotional and spiritual lives of women.

Servanthood versus Servitude

At the back of my daughter's baby book is a poem about how the housework will wait but the child won't—one of those "these days are precious" kinds of things. The poem suggests that a mom needs to let go of the idea that she can do everything and instead let her child be the most important thing in her life. That's perfectly legitimate advice, but eventually someone needs to wash the dishes.

When a woman becomes a mother, she begins performing a balancing act that is precarious at best. Whether she has a full-time job or stays at home with the kids, she has to find that fine line between caring for her children and caring for herself. While most Christians would at least give lip service to the idea that it's okay for a woman to set aside time to read her Bible or have coffee with a friend, the underlying message that her family comes first still remains. I know moms who truly can't find time to read a daily devotional because any free time is taken up with laundry, a shower, cleaning up the lunch mess, and paying the phone bill.

Motherhood does indeed take an unbelievable degree of selflessness—I've often thought the best way to teach abstinence in schools would be to let teenagers spend a weekend with a new mom. Believe me, I am convinced God changes the heart of a mother to allow her to willingly give up her sleep, her privacy, and her independence for the sake of her children, because I certainly wouldn't have the inner strength to do this on my own. Only true love could get a sleep-deprived new mother to wake up every two hours. Only true love keeps me sitting at the dining room table coloring with my daughter when I really need to clean the house before our small group comes over.

These are the necessary sacrifices we parents make every

day, and they are essential to the well-being of our children. But the "real" sacrifice, the kind that our evangelical culture tells us is truly required, is not found in these surface concessions to life with children. It is, as author Caryn Rubenstein puts it, "always worrying about what is best for the children, what will make them happiest, smartest, most secure. It means feeling guilty for not always being the most giving, supportive, caring mothers. It means making sacrifice a way of life."[1]

This is certainly the message of the church. When pastors, authors, and other church leaders tell us to make parenting our primary focus—and they tell us over and over—I am confident they don't intend to say that we should let our children take over our lives. And yet that's exactly what women hear when we are told to put our own needs aside for the sake of our children.

This idea is complicated for Christian women because we are taught—rightly so I believe—that the Christian life is all about servanthood and laying down our lives for others. There are few images of Christ's love as powerful as that of the suffering servant. In its best inception, we live out Christ's call to servanthood by humbly following God's path, not the world's. We serve our brothers and sisters by seeing that their needs are at least as important as our own and not thinking ourselves above loving the poor, the sick, the destitute. I believe that when most pastors and speakers and authors talk about Christians living lives of servanthood, that's what they mean.

However, what they mean and what women hear isn't always the same thing. I studied missions for a time in seminary. One of the first concepts future missionaries learn is that every culture has its own way of hearing the gospel; the images of God that mean one thing in our culture might mean something completely different in another. In other words, people can hear the same message in different ways.

The same is true for males and females. Research from the National Institute of Mental Health found that baby girls react much more dramatically to the distress of other babies than do baby boys. Our culture tells us that it's feminine to be nurturing and giving and to put others first, so that natural response to others turns into a gift for empathy. But our ability to recognize the needs of others is also what makes us so vulnerable to guilt and depression. We end up spending an extraordinary amount of emotional energy worrying about the well-being of the people we love.[2]

From a faith perspective, this shouldn't come as much of a surprise. Mary Stewart Van Leeuwen makes an excellent case for the idea that this extreme empathy is the result of sin.[3] Before the fall, Adam and Eve shared a relationship of equal dominion over creation and a true partnership as man and woman. However, when sin entered the world, the created order was set askew, and the traits of God manifested in humanity—our position of authority over the rest of creation and our desire to live in relationship with others—became distorted. As a result of sin, men tend to want to dominate relationships and women tend to bend over backwards to maintain them.

According to Van Leeuwen, "The particularly female sin is to use the preservation of . . . relationships as an excuse . . . to avoid taking risks. . . . Now this is a very seductive temptation indeed, for it so very easily masquerades as virtue. After all, don't Christians see self-sacrificing servanthood and the desire to maintain peace and social unity as fruits of the Holy Spirit . . . ? If women insist on peace at any price—if they settle for abnormal quietism as a way of avoiding the risk and potential isolation that may result from opposing evil—then they are not exhibiting the fruit of the Spirit. They are sinning just as surely as the man who rides roughshod over relationships in order to assert his individual freedom."[4]

That helps explain why when men hear a sermon on servanthood, it acts as a reminder of their sinful tendency to think of themselves first, to put their needs above those of others. A message about the importance of servanthood is an important reminder for men to resist their urge to dominate others. But when women, who already tend to sacrifice their own needs to those of others, are reminded to be servants, they hear that they aren't doing enough, that they are failing the most important people in their lives. So they dig in deeper, try harder, and work to subvert their needs even more.

A terrible cycle starts when a woman feels worn out and needs a break but is told that her need is less important than her child's need for her time and attention. Not only does that mother continue on past the point where her body and mind are asking for rest, she feels like a bad mother for even wanting that rest.

Granted, Andrea Yates had a mental illness that impacted her ability to reason clearly, but even before she moved into a psychotic state, she resisted the help she knew she needed because it would have made her look like a bad mother. After Yates's first suicide attempt, a mental health professional asked her what it was that was stressful in her life. Yates replied, "The kids. Trying to train them up right, being so young. It's a big responsibility and I don't want to fail."[5] For Yates, and too many other mothers, being a good mother means doing everything right, all the time, all alone. To ask for help, to admit to being worn down by motherhood and yearn for respite, to have prayed for

God's strength and wisdom and still feel inadequate, is the ultimate sign of failure.

Giving Our All

At the heart of these fears are our precious children. We believe the cult messages because we want desperately for our children to grow up to fulfill all the goodness and potential we see in them. We don't want them to suffer or make terrible mistakes or be hurt simply because we neglected to teach them some vital moral truth. We carry this responsibility with us more deeply than many of us can even articulate. Ironically, even as Christian women, we act as though we believe it will be our efforts, not God, that help our children grow into Christian adults. We put our needs aside in the hope that doing so will pay off when our children go on to do great things for the kingdom.

Caryn Rubenstein notes that,

The most fundamental assumption of all, the one that motivates and guides a sacrificial mother's every word and gesture, is that hers is the true sacrifice, the only one that really matters. In what may be her sole self-aggrandizing thought, she considers herself to be the only one who counts when it comes to her children's growth and ultimate happiness. With this attitude, of course, she sets herself up for terrible blame ten or fifteen years down the road. By the time her baby has become an unhappy teenager who's flunking English or using drugs, she's the only one who's at fault. And she accepts that blame wholeheartedly. Her first thought when anything goes badly for her child—from a broken arm to a lousy report card—will always be "What did I do wrong?"[6]

89

Ask any mother with a prodigal child and you'll find that she, at least in part, blames herself.

And so we throw ourselves into motherhood by giving up anything that impedes our ability to focus on our children in the hope that they turn out okay. The result, however, is that we sacrifice not only the selfish parts of ourselves but also those passions and desires that are legitimate expressions of who we are as children of God.

One of the women who filled out my survey wrote, "I had fairy tales like to be an actress or write a play or something. But the Lord has shown me that I have to let go and die to all of what I am even if it is a talent he has given me so that I can be His child and do all things to His glory only. That's not always easy and I have needed the support of my brothers and sisters in the Lord. To just tell me I should do those things would have got my focus on me and not on God. . . . I have had to and still do wrestle with wanting the attention being 'talented' would bring me, but that's not what pleases the Lord." She goes on to say that she has found an outlet for her creative side by being a good storyteller as she teaches children at her church, but that it's still difficult to push down her desire to use her gifts in other ways. I'm glad she feels God using her in the lives of children, but I hurt for this woman. She doesn't have a sense of peace about where she is in her life. She has a desire in her heart, a passion she knows was placed there by God, and yet she feels as if she can't use it. As a result, she's fighting to squelch her gifts because she believes that's the kind of sacrifice God requires of her.

Naturally, there are seasons in life when we do have to put our passions on hold for a time. I would love to be involved in a community theater or choral group, but I know I can't commit to two months of nightly rehearsals or a weekend of concerts during the Christmas season when my children are young. God has given me a sense of contentment with this, and I know that when the timing is right, God will open up the doors for me to express the gifts I've been given. My prayer is that my friend mentioned above will be given either a contented heart or a clear open door. Right now, she seems to have neither.

Other women (particularly the stay-at-home moms) wrote of their loneliness, their sense of isolation, their feelings of boredom and stagnation—all the result of giving up the things they used to enjoy in order to care for their children. Many said that they expected to have lots of time to talk with other mothers, but instead they feel more alone than ever. Traci says, "Now that most of my friends are on their second, third, or fourth child, there just isn't a lot of time for casual get-togethers. I scheduled lunch with a girlfriend for a month from now—and on a Sunday—because between the schedules of our combination of five children (two are infants) there wasn't any other time that would work. In the winter, it's nearly impossible to get together with other parents because someone's child is always sick!"

Even when we moms manage to get together, the conversations go something like this:

"So, how have you been? Isaac, please put that down."

"Oh, we're okay—hang on—Nina, do you need to go potty?"

"Wow, so she's potty training, huh?"

"We're working on it. How did . . . Nina, let Mommy tie your shoes so you don't trip. What was I going to ask you?"

By the time Isaac's fed up with sharing and Nina needs a nap, Mom and Mom have finished maybe two or three thoughts—and that's an in-depth conversation.

For many women, trying to get time away from the kids is nearly as stressful as being with them. I used to get together with a small group of moms for an informal "Moms' Night Out." Most of the women had already made dinner for their husbands and kids or at least given Dad specific instructions on who needed what.[7] Some couldn't meet until their nursing babies were asleep so they could get a good three-hour break before being on call again.

Frankly, even if these moments of female fellowship could be made more meaningful, the fact remains that they are too few and far between for them to truly alleviate the intense loneliness many mothers experience. Our friendships with other women are often the first thing we sacrifice when we have children, simply because we know they'll understand.

The impact social isolation has on a woman is often difficult for men to understand. But women truly are more social by nature, and we depend on relationships to maintain our sanity in life. Van Leeuwen explains that "the image of God includes sociability: God is intrinsically social: Creator, Redeemer and Holy Spirit working in cooperative interdependence throughout the whole of the biblical drama." Her argument is that our inbred social needs are really a reflection of the image of God in us as women. She goes on to say, "Feminist theologians and psychologists have pointed out that one of the chief features of a feminine perspective on life is a concern for relationships."[8]

The bottom line is that women need friendships, and not just with their children. To be whole, mothers need other adults in their lives. We are fed by our connections with other people. When those connections are severed, we lose a lifeline that's essential to our ability to function. God created all of us to live in fellowship, but for too many mothers, that desire to spend time supporting and being supported, talking and listening, laughing and crying, is pushed aside and deemed "selfish."

Focus on Something Else

Despite the parallels with servanthood, the evangelical emphasis on sacrifice as a maternal virtue is yet another motherhood ideal the church has borrowed from the secular culture. Remember the "republican mother" from the eighteenth century who saw it as her civic duty to subjugate her will to that of her child? That idea was ignored by the church for quite a while. In fact, it wasn't until after World War II that the conservative edge of American Protestantism began to put any emphasis at all on family life as a concern of the church.[9] Before that point, the liberal and mainline churches were participating in the secular conversations about the ways in which parenting styles and philosophies impacted children. For fundamentalist Christians, the focus of the church was on making disciples of the unchurched and leading believers to lives of piety. The fundamentalist movement operated on the fringes of the culture, not in consort with it. It was the conservatives who saw the liberal church's emphasis on the family as idolatrous.

However, by the late 1950s, mainline Protestants were beginning to move away from conversations about the Christian family ideal. The increase in the divorce rate as well as criticism that the church was too focused on the family nudged the mainline and liberal camps of the church to make a move to other issues.[10] Yet the popular culture was producing a growing body of literature for parents, such as Dr. Spock's book, which became the de facto parenting "bible" for mid-century parents.

Margaret Lambers Bendroth points out that in the vacuum left by the mainline shift to other issues, evangelicals "quickly advanced into the unoccupied territory, momentarily casting aside skepticism their fundamentalist forebears might have demanded. . . . The neoevangelical postwar revival joined mainstream America at its new center, a return to the traditional family. . . . In discussing the family, they clearly had uncovered a topic which all but guaranteed them an appreciative audience and a spot closer in from the margins of American society."[11]

Indeed, by the mid-'70s, Focus on the Family had begun its ministry and Jimmy Carter graced the cover of *Time* magazine with the headline, "The Year of the Evangelical." Making the family central to its message allowed the evangelical culture to become a player in the national conversation.

Understanding the history of the connection between the church and the family is essential if mothers are to get out from under the mistaken idea that our primary role as women and as Christians is to serve our children. We need to let go of this idea not only for our own sense of balance and wholeness but because it is not at home with the gospel. The loss of friends, of time alone, of sleep, of connection with the "outside" world leaves us in a state of suspended animation where life as we once knew it seems to be on hold until all the kids are in school and we have a bit of time to recover. But in those early years of giving ourselves over to our children, we risk losing more than social connections and a little of our sanity. We risk losing our ability to be people who seek to live out God's kingdom on earth.

The impact of the social disconnect is not just that women don't know what happens in the news each day or that we suffer from intense loneliness, it's that our view of the world becomes smaller. When our focus is on our families, we become blind to the needs of the world around us. We don't ignore them intentionally, but we tend to become so absorbed in the details of mothering that we often don't have the mental or spiritual space to care about the rest of the world in meaningful ways.

Living in the bubble of motherhood leaves us with a kind of tunnel vision that prevents us from seeing the work God would have us do in the world. I need to be clear on this because it's an idea I know can be greatly misunderstood. I don't mean to suggest that we not take mothering seriously. I also don't mean to suggest that we ignore the needs of our children in our efforts to follow God. I remember the story of a Christian singer who grew up the only child of parents who had a traveling singing ministry. She spent much of her childhood living out of a car, driving around the country, performing with her parents in small churches. She wasn't able to make the kinds of friends a child needs because she was rarely in the same place for long. She wasn't allowed to complain about her circumstances because she'd been taught that what her family was doing was "the Lord's work" and therefore not to be questioned. While she doesn't exactly resent her parents, she does say that she felt as though she was less important to them than this dream they had of spreading the gospel one tiny town at a time.

Opening ourselves up to life beyond our children doesn't have to mean that they become less important, rather that the rest of the world—the other children and families out there—becomes at least as important as our own flesh and blood. Loving our neighbors as ourselves means that we care what happens to orphaned children in Africa and pregnant teenagers in the suburbs and hungry men and women in the shelters. I truly believe that when God gives us both a family and a vision for kingdom work, God will help us find a way to keep both in balance and to successfully meet the needs of our children in the midst of our efforts at blessing the world. In the case of the singer mentioned above, I simply cannot believe that her situation was what God wanted for her or her family.

Here again, the word *call* tends to pop up, as in "I'm not called to missions, I'm called to motherhood." And I certainly recognize that heading to a foreign mission field is not feasible for every family. The church we attend sends members of our community to Guatemala for a week twice a year; Jimmy and I would love to go, but right now, a week feels like too much time away from our young children. But Van Leeuwen points out that family should never be an excuse for not obeying God's call on the lives of every one of us. She says, "Every Christian is a 'sent one' (the meaning of the Latin word from which mission is derived). In light of Pentecost, they are all called to proclaim the lordship of Christ and the healing and hope he offers, so that through active witness and self-sacrificing service to their fellow sinners, they may be drawn to God and share in the building up of his kingdom. All other callings—whether as wife or husband, married or single, clergy or laity—are merely secondary offices within this larger calling that all Christians share."[12]

Until we are able to go to Guatemala, Jimmy and I search for other ways to share our gifts with the world. He spends a day each month with one of his former students, a boy whose father is in prison and whose mother has her hands full with a full-time job and a chronically ill child. We have intentionally opened our home to people in need of a place to stay or food to eat. We work at being people who bring peace and justice to others in any way we can.

When Christ told us to go and make disciples of all nations, he didn't offer an exemption to mothers. The world is in great need of the love of God, and for us to live as though mothers are not necessary to the battle, that mothers should instead stick with influencing their two or three young charges who have a head start in life simply by living in families where they are loved and wanted and cared for, seems to me to run counter to everything Jesus taught.

A Case Study

When my friend Tessa was pregnant with her second child, I was invited to a different kind of shower for her. Before the invitation arrived, she assured me that the actual event wouldn't be as strange as it sounded.

The party was called a Blessing Way and rather than focus on the baby, we would focus on the mother. We were each asked to bring a small item that reminded us of Tessa or symbolized something about the unique gifts she brought to mothering. These tokens would then be attached to a blessing wreath she could bring with her to the delivery room as a source of strength during her labor. The invitation also mentioned poems and readings and a crown of flowers for Tessa to wear during the blessing. I agreed to go because I like Tessa; she said she wasn't quite sure what to expect either.

When I got to Tessa's house, a small group of women had gathered in the living room. I was a little late, and someone was already reading a letter from Tessa's mother, who couldn't be there. The letter was really lovely and full of encouragement for Tessa; it spoke of her inner strength, her kindness, her goodness, her faith in God. Her mom also included a few seashells to remind Tessa of the beauty and intricacy of the life that God was creating in her. Then each woman in the room took her turn sharing her words of support for Tessa and presenting a small symbol for the wreath. It was absolutely wonderful.

What set this event apart from the average baby shower wasn't just the lack of yellow blankets and outfits from BabyGap. It was that the focus was on the wonderment of motherhood itself. We weren't simply celebrating the fact that Tessa had successfully gotten pregnant and was about to give birth but that she was in the midst of a mysterious process of growing and changing as the result of this un-born child.

And in truth, we weren't just celebrating Tessa, we were promising to support her as a mother. Our gifts were our way of offering her a tangible sign of the gifts she brings to motherhood. Our words were our way of encouraging her that she was up to the task of raising this baby. Our presence was our way of telling her, "You're not in this alone."

I left the Blessing Way feeling privileged to be a woman, to be a mother. I left feeling as if I was part of a sisterhood of women who knew what it was to love another person with white-hot intensity.

This affirmation of sisterhood was the perfect antidote to the message that motherhood is somehow an individual, private act. A friend once asked me if I believed "all that 'it takes a village' bunk." Absolutely! Without a connection to other women, to other roles, to other passions, a woman becomes a shell of who she was created to be. When a woman is pushed out of "the village," she loses her ties to the very body of Christ of which she is an essential member.

7

THE STAY-AT-HOME MOTHER

I n the fall of 2002, my daughter came home from her first day of kindergarten and announced, "This was the best day of my whole life!" She then launched into a breathless twenty-minute monologue about her teacher's outfit, who got to walk to the cafeteria to collect the milk for the class, and how there was a goldfish and a dollhouse and a dress-up area in the room. As I listened to her, I kept thinking, *I'm so glad I'm here for this.*

I've been a stay-at-home (well, at least a work-at-home) mom for two years. In so many ways, the move from working full-time in the office to working part-time at home has been a tremendous blessing. I get to hear about Emily's day at school while she's still excited and eager to share every detail. I get to eat lunch with the cutest little boy who ever lived. I get to participate in the moments that fill my children's days and watch them grow and change. There's not a doubt in my mind that being home with them is good for all of us. But to tell you the truth, I have no doubt in my mind that my working in the office full-time was also good for all of us.

There is perhaps no greater pressure in Christian womanhood than the pressure to stay home with our children. Really, it's hard to argue with the idea that children do best when they are able to spend large chunks of time in the loving care of their parents. Children need quality and quantity time with people who think they are amazing. They need consistent affection and guidance from people they know and trust. They need adults who love them unconditionally, who will teach them how to function in the world, who are willing to pay attention to their needs and meet those needs in loving, appropriate ways. I would never suggest that parents are unnecessary to the well-being of their children.

At the same time, I'm convinced that the belief that none of this can happen unless a mother is home with her children is perhaps the mother of all motherhood myths. The expectation that the only godly mother is one who chooses not to work outside the home is the culmination of all the wrong-headed thinking about motherhood the church has promoted over the last fifty years.

Now that I'm at home, some aspects of my life have become much easier (no one cares what I wear), while others have become much more challenging (is it just my Isaac or are other little boys obsessed with flushing?). While the details of my days have changed, I don't believe that the life I am living now is somehow more faithful to the gospel than my life as a working mother. In fact, it could be argued that because I can go days without speaking to anyone outside of my immediate family, I have fewer opportunities to share God's love than I had when I went to the office every day.

On the surface, the evangelical emphasis on stay-at-home mothering fits right in with our understanding of the family as the primary venue for spiritual formation. The idea that a mother should be home with her children is consistent with the idea that a child's faith is indelibly shaped by his or her family. And for those who hold to the tabula rasa philosophy of development, it makes perfect sense that the person who spends the most time with a child will wield the most influence over the way that child turns out.

To make this argument even more cogent, the evangelical culture has added layers of theology to the conversation. The stay-at-home discussion quickly devolves into a discussion of women's roles, the dangers of day care, and the evil influence of feminism. In the minds of many evangelicals, there is a biblical mandate for women to stay home with their children. But in truth, it isn't biblical for evangelical culture to treat stay-at-home motherhood as the only expression of godly maternal love. That is not to say that a woman who feels God moving her to be home with her children is somehow letting down all of womankind or that she has chosen the "traditional" and therefore "oppressive" role of previous generations. On the contrary, I know many stay-at-home moms who are happy as clams to hang out with their kids, to not have the stress of working full-time while raising a family, to have the freedom to volunteer at their kids' schools, to chaperone field trips, to homeschool. But they're happy because they have full confidence that this is where God has placed them right now.

The Work of Motherhood

Someone once told me that the most wonderful place to live is at the intersection of our giftedness and God's involvement in the world. It's a perfectly healthy, normal, even biblical goal to want to spend our time and energy doing work that blesses the world. It's also healthy, normal, and even biblical to want to spend our time and energy using the passions and strengths God has given us to create these blessings.

We certainly live as though we believe this, spending years trying to determine what kind of work we'd like to do, praying for God to give us a sense of calling so we will find meaningful ways to use our gifts. Most of us would never stay in a job that was clearly a poor fit. For example, I would make an awful tax attorney. I am lousy with numbers and remembering rules and regulations. I would cave under the pressure of knowing that my work could make or break someone's entire financial future. I can't imagine God ever commanding me to be a tax attorney because it's quite clear that I was created with other gifts that God is using in other ways.

It's pretty obvious where I'm going with this. Mary Stewart Van Leeuwen points to the irony of limiting half the population to one kind of work when she says,

Christians believe in the uniqueness of each individual life—a belief that quite rightly undergirds their opposition to abortion on demand, for instance. But until recently this was a belief that was regularly qualified the moment a baby girl was born. When a boy was born, few people presumed to predict what kind of work he would be doing thirty years down the road. His options were considered numerous, limited only by his intelligence, motivation and (ideally) the kind of call God issued. But when it came to girls, many Christian parents forgot about created uniqueness, and about Pentecost and its implications [that all people are called to spread the gospel]. They assumed and even prayed for a successful career as wife and mother, and nothing else. Indeed, some still assume that God, by definition, can call their daughters to nothing else, and that to be single and female (or married, female and not a full-time homemaker) is somehow to have failed, morally and spiritually.[1]

The same can be said for women who *do* stay home with their children only to find that they don't like it very much. They are told that the life they are living is God's best for them, the life they are meant to lead. But caring for children all day is more draining and more difficult than most women ever expect. Even women who can't wait to be at home, those who have dreamed of motherhood since their own toddler days, often have moments of wanting to run away from home. Most churches are unaware of the real emotional and spiritual needs of stay-at-home mothers. They do not recognize that a woman might feel anything other than tremendously blessed by the experience of being home with her children.

The Faithful Mother

One of the primary reasons Christians feel strongly that mothers should be home with their children is so that we can teach them the things of faith. We rightly take the mandate to pass on God's commands "when you sit at home and when you walk along the road, when you lie down and when you get up" (Deut. 11:19) very seriously. For evangelicals, this passage suggests that we must never miss an opportunity to pass on our faith to our children, that it is the job of parents to do so. But we have allowed this sense of responsibility to become twisted into an intense pressure to make sure that not a moment is wasted. For a mother to leave her children in the care of someone else while she works outside the home is for her to risk an opportunity to instill godly values in her children. A mother who stays home is there to take advantage of the teachable moments that come along and therefore ensure that her children will hold fast to the faith.

The truth of the Deuteronomy passage is that children learn from us as they see us live our faith in all times and in all places. There is no suggestion here for mothers to stay home. There is no suggestion that mothers—and only mothers—are responsible for the faith of their children. Our job is to teach them, yes, but isn't it possible for a child to learn about faith from a mother who holds down a job? Certainly fathers are included in this command, but I have yet to hear an evangelical encourage fathers to stay home. (There's some irony in the idea that evangelicals believe parents, particularly fathers, are the teachers of faith, and yet it is mothers who are told to stay home.)

All this pressure to be not only the primary provider of love and affection and discipline and guidance but also of faith formation can crush even the most enthusiastic mother. When the spiritual guide hat is added to the stay-at-home mother's wardrobe, she is destined to fail. After all, how can you measure your ability to instill faith in another person? How can you know what the Holy Spirit is up to in a child's life? How can you guarantee that all the creativity and energy and fervent prayer you pour into a child will result in a faith-filled adult? You can't. And while we all know that parenting is never an "if/then" proposition (as in "If your kids love Jesus, then they won't give in to peer pressure"), women continue to get the message that there is a right way to raise our children and that our children's failures are really our failures as their mothers. Alana notes,

"I know God has given me a huge responsibility to raise my children and not hinder their faith. I know I'm supposed to train them in the ways of the Lord, but I don't know how to do it. It feels like one more area where I'm failing."

As I did research for this book, I wandered through a few Christian bookstores to see what kinds of resources are available for women. I was amazed at how dour life looks from the women's section. The shelves are filled with books that remind us of all the ways we fail to live up to the mythical standard of the godly woman. There are books on how to parent better, love better, look better, clean better, pray better, cook better, relate better, and sleep better. It's not enough that our evangelical culture tells us to stay home, it is determined to remind us of how completely unprepared we are to do motherhood well. What's worse, there is little truly Christian about the mass of expectations placed on the shoulders of stay-at-home mothers.

A Modern Model

In reality, the ideal of the stay-at-home mother whose primary task is to care for her children is only about fifty years old and is almost exclusively a middle-class, Western concept. In the pre-industrial era, a man or a woman holding anything we would call a "job" was the exception, not the rule. The majority of families lived on farms or in rural areas where every adult, regardless of gender, needed to contribute to the survival of the family. Until the mid-1900s, American women not only worked, they had very little choice in the matter. During the Depression, anyone who could find work worked. During the two world wars, women held the economy together by filling in at factories, hospitals, and businesses while the men were overseas.

A few years ago, PBS broadcast a series called "Frontier House." The premise was for three families to re-create life in the American frontier. For several months, the families had access only to those materials and services that would have been available to pioneer families. That meant no running water, no electricity, no power tools, no cars. While this experiment was interesting on many levels, what was most striking to the women involved was just how much work it took to maintain a household.

The women who had children to feed would wake up around 5:00 a.m. to grind the flour, milk the cow, churn the butter, and start the fire. The simple act of making biscuits for breakfast was a two-hour affair, and that was just the morning routine! Laundry took days. Running out of water was a crisis. A change in the weather could mean the difference between having fresh vegetables or stale bread for dinner. There was certainly no time for making smiley-face sandwiches or planning creative family Bible studies. These women may have been home, but with their fifteen-hour workdays and endless lists of chores, they couldn't be less like the modern ideal of the stay-at-home mother. Certainly no one would argue that these women were somehow less godly, less loving toward their children than those of us who just happen to be born into an age when we have the luxury of leisure time to spend with our children.

My grandmother raised seven daughters. She was a stay-at-home mother, but her days were absorbed with sewing, cooking, cleaning, ironing, farming, and cooking some more. Just keeping the house running was more than a full-time job. She was more of a working mother than I'll ever be.

The belief that God wants mothers to devote themselves

to their children to the exclusion of other kinds of work also falls apart when we look at the way other cultures function. In primitive societies, women may have their children nearby as they tend the fires, weave the baskets, or collect the water, but their focus is on keeping the tribe alive. Even in cultures where the gospel has been embraced, the work of women rarely changes. Their contribution to the community is essential to its survival. If God's best is for women to dedicate themselves to the care of their children, wouldn't God make it possible for all women, regardless of their nationality, to do so?

Then there are single mothers for whom staying at home is rarely an option. It's interesting to me that most evangelicals allow for single mothers to work outside the home because these women have to, as though necessity somehow trumps living by the "Christian" standard. If we really believe children are better off with a parent at home, it would make more sense for the church to find ways to subsidize single-parent families so the mother could stay home with her children, who are already at a loss for having only one parent. If that sounds laughable to you, consider that this is exactly what welfare was designed to do: give poor parents the financial help they needed so they could raise their children in a healthy environment.

Often the very Christians who believe that mothers should be at home decry the welfare state and insist that those who can work should. I've never been able to figure out why there are those who insist that mothers stay home with their children unless they are poor, in which case they better go out and get a job to support their children. If I have this straight, we're saying that poor children, who already have a major strike against them, don't need their mothers as much as middle- and upper-class children who often come from two-parent families and go to good suburban schools. And this makes sense how?

The contemporary model of the stay-at-home mother is clearly a blip on the screen of women's history. Surprisingly, it's also little more than a blip in the overall story of evangelicalism. In the early days of the fundamentalist movement, the role of women, when discussed at all, was in the context of our work in the church, not the family. The fundamentalists actually distanced themselves from conversations about women's roles in the home because that was seen as a primarily secular discussion.

But as the popular conversation continued, the fundamentalists felt pulled into the fray. It was then, a mere sixty-some years ago, that evangelicals actually laid out an expectation for a woman's role in the family. Margaret Lamberts Bendroth notes, "In strict, hierarchical language—terminology generally missing from fundamentalist discussions of women's roles before the 1940s—writers insisted that the 'scriptural home' placed men at the top of a ladder of command. The consistently embattled tone of this writing suggests that fundamentalists adopted this ethic with difficulty, and that its standards of feminine submission had never been normative for the movement as a whole."[2] Clearly, the model of motherhood that so many of us labor to live with is not really a biblical idea at all but a cultural expectation that is younger than most of our parents.

Still, there are those who will insist that the Bible is very clear about the need for mothers to be home with their children. But in his book *10 Lies the Church Tells Women*, J. Lee Grady points out that it's a mistake to interpret the Bible as saying women shouldn't work outside the home for the simple reason that working outside the home was a concept women in Bible times didn't ever deal with. Paul wouldn't have written to the Ephesians or Titus or Timothy in an effort to get women to return to their proper place in the home because they were already there. Grady says, "We cannot use these verses to imply that Paul's command to 'keep house' or to be 'workers at home' requires that all Christian women in the 21st Century stay in their kitchens all day or shun their God-ordained career paths. Those who teach this view impose a cruel and legalistic burden on women that isn't supported by Scripture."[3]

To call staying at home a burden might sound a bit strong, but considering the emotional and spiritual toll being the primary parent can bring, Grady is not necessarily overstating the impact of the cult of the family.

Case Study

One of the biggest challenges for mothers who work outside the home is finding quality childcare. While the mommy wars often make working mothers out to be self-centered careerists who give little thought to the well-being of their children, the truth is that the question of who will care for their children while they work is one that obsesses every working mother I know.

My friend Suzanne is an elementary school teacher. In the two years since she had her son, she has gone through four different childcare arrangements ranging from a large daycare center to a one-on-one babysitting situation. During the course of those two years, I watched Suzanne wrestle with the guilt of leaving her baby in a room full of other babies, agonize over conversations with the woman who cared for Suzanne's son in her home and who seemed overwhelmed by the responsibility, and cry over the lack of suitable choices available for her.

Eventually she found a woman near the school where she teaches who has a licensed in-home day care. Suzanne and her son both love this woman, and Suzanne has had several months of peace over her choice. But she is now pregnant with baby #2. Since her current day-care provider doesn't take infants, she is starting the painful process all over again. (Before you decide she'd be better off quitting her job, please reread this chapter and keep in mind that quitting isn't an option—or even a desire—for many women.)

For many Christians, childcare has become one of the great evils of modern life. It is a sure sign that the modern family is under attack and that the next generation of children will pay dearly for the selfishness of their money-hungry parents. But those people haven't met Debbie Johnson.

Debbie was our babysitter when I worked full-time in the office. She cared for Emily for more than four years, and for Isaac once he arrived. Not only was I confident that my children were in good hands, which reduced my stress level significantly, but she became an invaluable part of my children's emotional, physical, and spiritual development.

Debbie truly loves children, and my children were the beneficiaries of her great affection. When Emily was a baby, Debbie delighted over her daily accomplishments—rolling over, cruising the furniture, babbling along to Veggie Tales songs. She treated Emily—and later Isaac—with the same tenderness and patience she gave her own children. She taught Emily how to knead bread dough, something I couldn't have taught her even if I'd been home all day. She introduced Emily to her parents, two wonderfully kind people who became one more set of grandparents for my daughter. She included Emily in various outings with her homeschool co-op. One horrible week when Jimmy and I both had the flu, she not only cared for the perfectly healthy Emily but made homemade soup for the sickies. Our whole family adored her.

None of what Debbie did diminished my influence on my kids. On the contrary, I believe she reinforced my influence by lovingly instilling the same values in her home that we worked to instill in ours. She showed them every day that they were wonderful treasures worthy of her attention and affection. She became one more caring adult in the lives of my kids, one more positive influence on their lives, one more amazing model of God's love and care. And what child doesn't benefit from that?

Loving, caring childcare isn't one of the devil's tools. The positive influence of other adults can bring richness and variety to the life of a child. Rather than see childcare as a detriment to family life, we need to recognize that it can often be a tremendous blessing for parents *and* children.

If the church truly believes the best possible situation is for women to stay home with their children, then we should be actively involved in making staying at home possible for all women who want that opportunity. Those of us who believe mothers ought to be free to follow God's leading in their lives (even if that leads them to a job) have a vested interest in making life for stay-at-home mothers more viable, particularly when it comes to the economic toll of being a one-income family.

There are plenty of ways for Christians to effect changes that would benefit all mothers and allow women who want to be home the option of doing so. I don't necessarily mean holding on to welfare (although I find it interesting that the government has often been more proactive than the church in helping poor women care for their children). Consider the three-year paid maternity leave offered in some European countries or the idea of a tax break for families where the mother is staying home with her children.[4] It is possible for our society to become more mother friendly, and those of us who believe mothers are important ought to be doing all we can to help it become so.

8

THE REAL LIFE
OF AN
AT-HOME MOTHER

If modern mothers ever had an enemy, it is June Cleaver. Perhaps more than anyone else in history, June created in us the idea that the good mother spends her day happily meeting the needs of her family. She cooks a hearty breakfast, keeps a tidy house, and welcomes her weary charges home each afternoon with a plate of warm cookies and a tender smile. We never see June complain or wish for a more fulfilling role. We never see her sigh when she finally gets a minute to sit down only to be interrupted by yet another request from the Beav. She certainly never asks Ward to watch the boys for a night because she wants to go out for some "mommy time." June is the superhuman mother who sets us all up for disappointment.

The cult of the family has hijacked June as its mascot and made her even more inimitable by adding the weight of a child's spiritual well-being to June's already heavy load. Christian mothers today are expected not only to polish and iron and fix and fuss but to plan creative family devotions, volunteer to teach Sunday school, homeschool the kids, and build a family life that models the very heart of God.

Part of what makes the stay-at-home conversation so loaded is that women themselves often have conflicting feelings about their choice. Even mothers who love being home have days when they wish they were somewhere else. Traci told me, "After my first son was born, I telecommuted for a few months. During that time God really changed my heart. I realized that I would rather sacrifice the career I loved than sacrifice those early years with my young child. This is not to say that staying home was an easy choice for me. I missed work so much that sometimes it physically hurt. It took me a long time to be able to say with conviction, 'I stay home,' and to feel good about it." My friend Anna said, "On the whole, I love being a mom. It has its frustrations, but I never doubt that I am happier doing this than I was at my desk job. Being a mom often is not very intellectually stimulating, but then my job was very seldom intellectually stimulating."

Certainly being home with our children can be deeply satisfying, and I don't mean to suggest that it is hard and frustrating all day, every day. But the beautiful part of motherhood gets talked about all the time, particularly in Christian literature. What doesn't get addressed often enough is that along with the wonder and delight of raising children come intense challenges that can leave women emotionally raw.

On the surface, our Christian culture has begun to acknowledge the difficulties of being a stay-at-home mother. A whole new crop of books on the Christian market caters to the stressed-out mother and encourages her to lean on God through this often-trying season of life. But those books never address the idea that perhaps being a stay-at-home mom is difficult for some women because we have heaped an impossible load of expectations on Christian mothers, expectations that are bound to be dashed.

Traci wrote, "When women head into motherhood thinking it's going to be all flowers and sunshine, they're setting themselves and their children up for disappointment. One of my friends, who planned to stay at home with her child, returned to work after less than a year because staying home didn't meet her expectations. How *could* it?"

The thinking in the cult of the family also assumes that every woman knows how to mother, that the care and nurturing of children is something that comes naturally to anyone with breasts. But Alana, the mother of two preschoolers, notes, "I don't feel I have natural skills and abilities as a mom. I take care of their physical needs and keep the house organized and running smoothly, but I don't always know how to relate to my kids. Some women are just really natural with kids—even kids who aren't their own. They can talk with them and know how to prevent or quiet their tantrums. They seem to enjoy playing with them. I envy their gifts with children."

The emotional and spiritual toll of stay-at-home motherhood is tremendous. The stay-at-home moms I surveyed spoke of the loneliness, boredom, and depression that come with hanging around with kids for hours at a time and from the constant sense of not being up to the challenge of raising a human being. Anna wrote, "It can be very isolating being at home all day without any other adult interaction. I can usually handle it for a day or two at a time, but I have to make a point to get out of the house and see other people at least a couple of times a week, otherwise I start to feel kind of crazy." Alana says, "I got blindsided by the responsibility, the emotional ties, the worry, the exhaustion, the discipline issues, and the day-to-day care of children. The reality for me is that motherhood is very draining and tiring and humbling. On a regular basis I feel like a failure as a mom. My walk with the Lord has suffered since I became a mom. Spending time with God feels like another obligation—just one more person wanting something from me."

Nora's two children are adults now, but she says, "One of the greatest frustrations of my early years of parenting was having to put my dreams on hold. It was humbling, boring, tiring, and lonely at times (actually a lot of the time). What most stimulated and satisfied me was often not possible to have in my life. It felt like a wilderness wandering time when I learned my hardest lessons about being a servant. I felt—and still do feel—incredibly insecure about entering my parenting journey. Even to this day I think it's God's grace that has allowed my kids to become the people they are."

These are the women sitting in our churches, the women who are doing their best with very little rest or support. These are the women we are telling to do more and to do it better. And we are killing them.

Spoiled Rotten Mothers

Sadly, so many of us hide our sense of disappointment and our discontent with our lives as stay-at-home mothers because we've been taught that this is the life God wants for us, that to want something more is selfish and worldly. We are afraid to admit that our lives aren't what we hoped for because to do so would be to reveal some deep moral flaw. That fear isn't irrational. Unfortunately, it gets reinforced on a regular basis.

In a recent article in *The Christian Century,* writer Debra Bendis reviewed four secular books on motherhood. Each of the books discussed the "hidden" side of motherhood; the stress, the loneliness, the fears, the superwoman complex, and so on. In her discussion of Naomi Wolf's *Misconceptions,* Bendis notes that Wolf is whiney and seems very caught up in her own life—a critique of the book I've seen in other places. But she then launches into a paragraph that left me gasping. She wrote,

> While [young professionals] have been able to achieve much in a professional world, which supplies a social life as well as a career, they seem not to have developed the capacities for family life. They seem never to have learned about sewing, gardening, cooking or puttering—the "soft" activities that can make home a comfortable and welcome place instead of a prison of isolation. They may have prepared the occasional gourmet meal for 12, and can find the best price for a Club Med vacation, but they have never prepared three meals a day, or abandoned the gym for walks through the neighborhood. Without a habit of being at home, the mayhem of a toddler lunchtime or the tedium of a rainy day makes a day at work look like rescue—while home is only a punishment.[1]

I read this paragraph about six times to make sure I'd understood her correctly. And I kept thinking, *Is she kidding?* Does she honestly believe a mother's happiness rests in her sewing skills or that "puttering" is a cure for depression? Does she really think that moms who stay at home enjoy rainy-day tedium? Does she really think that stay-at-home moms run to Target once a week because they have to and not because they need to break up the day by getting out of the house and strapping their toddlers into a cart for a while?

Her assumption is that women who dare to be unhappy or less-than-fulfilled by making Easy Mac and reviewing spelling tests for days on end are spoiled princesses who miss their big-shot jobs and corner offices. While it's true that many stay-at-home moms, myself included, think back fondly on the working-girl perks of hour-long lunches and coworkers who notice when you get your hair cut, it's ludicrous to assume that holding down jobs before we became mothers somehow ruined our ability to be happy homemakers.

I think Bendis's statement is also inaccurate, at least as it relates to Christian women. Rather than puttering and gardening and cooking being the keys to our happiness, they are, for many women, the bane of our existence. If anything, we put too much emphasis on creating a perfect home complete with handmade centerpieces and memory books filled with theme stickers and cropped pictures of the kids at the beach. There is tremendous pressure to prove to the world that we are capable of caring for our families if only to show the secular culture that this is the life that comes from living obediently. To fail at this is to fail at God's plan.

Stay-at-home motherhood truly is a mission, one into which not all of us are led. Those who are need constant support and opportunities for respite. Yes, there are many deeply fulfilling moments in the life of a stay-at-home mom; sitting across from my newly minted kindergartener is one I will never forget. But our days are often tedious, harrowing, and intensely frustrating. What we need from the church is not a set of unreasonable expectations but encouragement and prayer that God will keep giving us endless reserves of patience, compassion, wisdom, and love. We need other adults in our lives who are willing to listen when we need to vent, who will take the kids at the drop of a hat, and who will occasionally ask our opinion on something other than potty training. We need to know that we are free to listen to God's voice and follow God's leading—whether that is into our homes or into an office. We need to know that our efforts at parenting well are covered by God's rich grace and that, whether we stay at home or head to work, it is God, and God alone, who will fill our children with all that they need to love and serve in God's name.

A Case Study

I have so many inspiring stay-at-home moms in my life that my next book might have to be a Christian mom's version of "Profiles in Courage." There's Jen, who is trained as an early childhood education specialist and sees her life as a stay-at-home mother of two preschoolers as her "lab." She says, "When I do go back to teaching, I'm going to have such a different perspective because I've learned so much from my children." There's Marci, who is writing her first novel during her toddler's nap times and strikes me as the most patient human being alive. And there's my sister-in-law, Libby, who is the master of balancing her kids' needs with her own. She is committed to her Bible study and her volunteer work at the school but equally committed to making sure her children get to experience everything from art classes to electric guitar lessons. Libby has figured out how to schedule time with her husband, time for herself, and time with friends without sacrificing her relationship with her children. She might spend her day on the go, but she is incredibly close to her three kids and they are growing into fantastic people.

For me, though, the most inspiring stay-at-home mom I know is my dear friend Jill. Jill, the mother of two preschoolers, is a strong Christian. To me, she captures the spirit of what stay-at-home mothering can look like when women are allowed to listen to God's voice, given permission to find ways to fill their souls with meaningful non-mothering activities, and empowered to use their gifts in the church and the community as well as in their families.

Jill used to work in advertising sales and was terrific at it. She moved up very quickly in every company she worked for. She loved meeting clients, pitching ideas, and closing the deal. Jill shared her faith with innumerable work contacts and built a reputation for being a wonderful, strong, accomplished woman with a stellar future.

However, when Jill became a mother, she didn't hesitate to step off her career track. She could have been the head of sales at a major city newspaper, but she wanted to be home. Her family income could easily be twice what it is, but she wanted to be home. She could be enjoying the thrill of the sale, the power of being an influential player in a big city, the sense of fulfillment that comes from doing something she's very good at, but she wanted to be home. She says, "If I were working, I'd have great feedback, would enjoy the money, would have more tolerance for the kids because of the break, but God has clearly said 'No' for right now. When the kids are in school, God may have a different plan, but today, he clearly guides me to be with my children."

Jill would also be the first to admit that being at home with children can be intensely challenging, that there are days she wonders what on earth she's doing trying to raise children. She told me, "I expected myself to be more patient, more understanding, to be able to set long- and short-term goals and have a plan for getting there with my children. Sometimes the days are very long. But I believe that my ministry first is to raise my children to have a love for God and to grow them in godly character, much of which is done through my relationship with Christ and my marriage."

While Jill has chosen to give up a job she loved for now, she has kept herself open to the new ways in which God can use her during her time as a stay-at-home mom. Jill has trained for and run several marathons (I don't know how she does it either!), time she uses for prayer and fellowship with another running mom.

Jill has also discovered a gift for teaching. She and her husband met another couple through his job, and the wife expressed an interest in Christianity. Jill offered to do a Bible study with the woman once a week to help her learn more about God. In time, the study grew to include a few other women. Now, Jill's Bible study includes three separate groups of women and three rooms of childcare to watch the twenty-five children who come with their mothers. Jill says, "I never would have initiated such administrative work, but God's grown me with the call, while still growing me as a leader."

What's interesting about Jill's involvement in running and in organizing the Bible study is that neither activity is directly connected to her children. But for Jill, devoting some of her time and energy to these pursuits teaches her children something valuable. She says, "I feel like both of these areas—the running (exercise) and the small groups (fellowship)—are good for my kids to witness and emulate themselves as they grow. I feel like I'm modeling a lifestyle, not just doing what I want."

Jill is happy because she is in the place God has led her,

not because she has been forced to make a choice that doesn't fit her. She has kept herself open to the ways in which God can continue to use her many gifts both in her family and in her community. Her church has encouraged her desire to use her talents and passions to disciple others and has given her the freedom to explore all the ways God can use her. Jill has continued to listen carefully for God's voice to guide her as she moves forward in motherhood, with the belief that there will never be one and only one role for her as a child of God.

9

THE WORKING MOTHER

I recently had lunch with a woman whose children are now in their twenties. As I was telling her about this chapter, she asked, "Are the mommy wars still going on?" "Oh yeah," I said.

I have to admit that in some ways, it seems ridiculous that this chapter is even necessary anymore. I'd like to think there is really just a small sector of the Christian community that still believes women have no business working outside the home. I'd like to think people are smart enough to recognize that our society depends on working mothers and that if mothers didn't work, the massive labor shortages in schools, hospitals, factories, banks, and airports would lead to a shutdown of basically every service we depend on to keep our society running. I'd like to think no one really believes that all working mothers are in it for the money. But that's not the case.

Perhaps more than any other issue, the working mom/stay-at-home mom question has become the continental divide of Christian motherhood: Those at home move in one direction, and those with outside jobs move in another. Sadly, the twain rarely meet, in large part because the church has failed to incorporate mothers who work outside the home. As my friend Amanda, a working mother of a nine-year-old, says, "The church has this vision of what a Christian mom looks like, and it doesn't include the idea that she might be gone during the day."

Ministry resources aimed at working mothers are slowly increasing, but it is still the norm for women's fellowship groups to meet during the day, for sermons to assume that women are the primary caretakers of the children, and for books and seminars for women to concentrate on our role as wives and mothers rather than on professional development, faith in the workplace, or leadership training. While it's becoming less common for a Christian mother working outside the home to meet flat-out criticism for holding a job—although it still happens—there remains a lingering sense that she is an anomaly.

In truth, working mothers—even Christian working mothers—are increasingly the norm, not the exception. At *CPT*, we do a great deal of demographic research to determine who reads the magazine, what their lives are like, and what their needs are. We survey our subscribers several times a year and on each survey ask the subjects about their work status. For the last five years, our results have varied little: Roughly half of our readers (98 percent of whom are women) work more than twenty hours outside the home per week, while the other half either don't work at all or work less than twenty hours. Our readers are typical, conservative evangelical women. The majority are Baptist or involved in nondenominational Bible churches. More than 90 percent are on their first marriage, and more than 80 percent of them have children under the age of ten. They are extremely active in their churches and are deeply committed to the spiritual development of their children. And yet the number of them who work outside the home is not all that different from the number of working women in the general population (according to the 2000 Census, 58 percent of women nationwide are in the labor force). When it comes to working outside the home, there is little difference between Christian women and women in general.

It's safe to say that the question of whether Christian women should work outside the home has become irrelevant. Rather than focusing its energies on convincing women that they belong at home, thereby heaping minivan loads of guilt on women who are doing their best to manage their many roles, the church needs to focus on understanding the spiritual and emotional needs of women who work outside the home.

Why Women Work

In my experience, the second-most popular argument against working women (the first of course is that God tells them not to) is that their doing so means they have put their own needs—for financial comfort and material goods, for self-esteem and the desire to be "noticed" by society—above the well-being of their children. Honestly, of all the working women I know, not one of them is in it for these reasons.

Laurie is the mother of two. She also works full-time—a few days a week at home and two in the office. She says, "I truly believe that God gives all of us our 'marching orders.'

Some he calls to be full-time, play-on-the-floor moms, and others he calls to be moms-with-another-job moms. I love being a mom and I'm thrilled God has given me the privilege of raising these two great kids. However, I don't think he's created me to be a 'professional' mom. I love being with my kids, watching them grow, helping them learn. But I find so much more satisfaction and fulfillment when I edit a manuscript than when I build a Lego house or dress (and redress) Barbie for her eighty-seventh wedding. This has little to do with my role as a mom, but more to do with the gifts and talents God has given to me personally."

My friend Kate is the mother of three children under eight and a teacher who job shares with another teacher, meaning she works two to three days a week. She says, "My teaching job is good for many reasons. It is an outlet for interaction with colleagues and children other than my own. I am able to use the gifts that God has given me for teaching. It is an opportunity to challenge myself professionally to grow." Kate and her husband live in a modest house, drive modest cars, take modest vacations. It's hard to find anything selfish in Kate's motivation for working outside the home. Yet Kate has felt a definite bias against working mothers. She says, "In one Bible study I was involved in, there was a real feeling that moms who worked were less godly than the moms who stayed home."

The evangelical church does make some allowances for women to work. If a family is in dire financial straits and the mother is willing and able to contribute to the family income, few churches would counsel her to forgo work for the good of her children. More and more evangelical stay-at-home moms are working from home as writers, memory book or cosmetic consultants, or providing in-home day care (don't even get me started on the irony) in order to keep the family afloat. Other mothers work second- or third-shift jobs so they can be home with the kids while Dad's at work but still bring in needed money. It's hard to imagine any pastor criticizing these incredibly hardworking women who live on little sleep and virtually no downtime. But what about women who work because we want to?

I find that many Christian working mothers feel an intense need to justify their situation because they assume they're going to be criticized if they don't have a "good" excuse for working. It's as though financial need is the only legitimate reason for a person to leave her children during the day. To admit that we like working, that we could give it up but choose not to, is to open ourselves up to charges of selfishness, greed, and misplaced values. For some women, the desire to work outside the home might very well come from these places, but I don't know any of those women. There's this image of the ambitious, driven businesswoman who doesn't care what happens to her kids as long as she's successful at work, but I have truly never met her.

Another part of the working mother picture that doesn't get talked about much is the role of giftedness in the life of a working mom. Christian women often work outside the home because we believe we have gifts that God can use in the world. I want to be very clear. I know full well that God doesn't *need* me to do anything. I also know full well that God is using me in the lives of my children and that God didn't make a mistake by bringing Emily and Isaac into my life. I don't think motherhood is a waste of my gifts. I don't think there's something "better" than being a mother (although there are days . . .).

The Bible is clear that God gifts women in the same ways in which God gifts men (the biblical lists of gifts never specify gender) and that the Great Commission is given to all Christians, not just men or those women who happen to be child-less. I fully believe that I am just as called as anyone else to do what I can to bless the world in the name of Christ. I don't find any biblical free pass that excuses me from sharing God's love with the world simply because I have children. In fact, it seems to me that when God puts me in a position where my God-given gifts and passions and abilities can impact the lives of a few hundred thousand people and makes it possible for me to still be a faithful parent, the Christian thing to do is to make the most of that opportunity.

I'm not suggesting that God wants all women to work any more than I think God wants all women to stay home. But I am convinced that the primary call on the lives of all Christians is to live faithfully in every realm in which God places us. I am equally convinced that if God sends us down a path and we continue to seek God's guidance and wisdom as we walk down that path, God will make sure that our children won't suffer because of it.

My friend Renee is a religion professor who shapes the worldview of hundreds of college students each day. It's hard for me to believe that God would rather she give up that opportunity to focus all her efforts solely on her two daughters. Indeed, Renee is an incredible mother whose daughters are caring, compassionate, and very bright. They will grow up knowing that they are loved but also that God can use them in the world just as God has used their mother.

Making Room for Daddy

When Emily was almost two, I had to go to a weekend youth conference to represent *Campus Life* magazine. The conference was in Minneapolis, near my hometown, so Jim and Emily came with me, and my parents drove to the Twin Cities to spend the weekend with us.

During the conference, I had the chance to chat with the main speaker, a man about my age who had a real heart for teenagers. We talked about parenting and marriage and all the usual stuff. He told me that his wife was nine months pregnant with their second child and that she and their two-year-old were home. He told me some "funny" little story about how she had called him because she'd gotten locked out of the house and didn't know where he'd put the spare key.

He then went on to question me about my decision to keep working, despite having a young child. "You work full-time? Where is your daughter when you're at work?" "Isn't that hard on your family?" There was a slightly accusatory tone in his voice as he asked me about the reasons I was still working and leaving my child in the care of someone else.

While part of me wanted to tell him this was none of his beeswax, the rest of me was thinking about his very pregnant wife, home alone with a toddler while her husband spent every weekend for the better part of three months on the road. Why, I wanted to ask, was it okay for him to work all week and leave his family every weekend? Wasn't that a little hard on *them?*

All kinds of assumptions get in the way of the church's acceptance of Christian working mothers: the assumption that God wants them home, that they work because of greed and selfishness, that they have chosen their careers over their families. Underneath all of these assumptions is the idea that women are uniquely suited to caring for children. Since the Bible is very clear that parents have an important role in the spiritual formation of their children, I can see how it makes sense for some people to believe that the more "gifted" parent—the mother—should spend the maximum amount of time possible raising them.

I don't know about your family, but my husband would be the first to tell you—and I'd be the first to agree—that he is at least as good a parent as I am, if not better, in many ways. He has more energy for running around, he is often more patient, and with two master's degrees—one in pastoral counseling and the other in special education—he knows much more about child development, conflict resolution, and basic psychology than I do. If I had to pick one of us to be the primary caregiver in our family, it would be Jim.

When Emily was a baby, Jim worked flextime and went to work at noon, so he and Emily hung out all morning. Their time together forged an amazing bond between them. Jim knows Emily's temperament, he knows her schedule, he knows how to calm her and care for her and soothe her. If she wakes up scared in the middle of the night, he can snuggle her back to sleep as easily as I can. He and Isaac are close—Jim is still an active, intentional dad—but we've both noticed that Isaac seems more attached to me because I'm home with him all day and Jim isn't. Frankly, we both miss sharing the parenting load a bit more evenly.

I know many families where the father is deeply involved in the lives of his children. My friend Alex worked a flextime schedule three days a week so he could pick up his daughters after school on those days when his physician wife couldn't. He often ran them to after-school activities, did the grocery shopping with them, made their dinner (real food, too, not just hot dogs and chips), gave them their baths, and got them ready for bed so their mom could just hang out with them when she got home. His strong presence in their lives certainly hasn't taken away from their close relationship with their mother. Instead, the girls have tight bonds with both of their parents. How can you argue with that?

Now that my dad is a grandfather, he often comments on how much he regrets not being more involved in the lives of his children. Back in the '60s and '70s when my brother and I were growing up, dads went to work and moms took care of the kids. Everyone my parents knew lived that way, so it never occurred to them to do anything different. Now my dad watches Jim play with our children, make them lunch, handle their discipline issues, change Isaac's diapers, and help Emily figure out how to share her coloring book. Dad sees that Jim has a bond with our kids that he didn't have with my brother and me when we were young. Sure, we found other ways to get close to our dad, and both my brother and I love him dearly, but Dad feels as if he missed out on something precious in not being more intentional in his relationship with us.

Undoubtedly, some women are better at caring for their children than their husbands are, but I believe that's primarily a socialization issue, not a genetic, gender-related given. The tangential fallout of the church's stance on stay-at-home mothering is that it's aced fathers out of the chance to build unbreakable bonds with their children. It could even be argued that the Christian men's movement (i.e., Promise Keepers, the Wild at Heart seminars) is really just a course correction made necessary by the church's stringent understanding of gender roles.

A Case Study

Working mothers are often criticized for trying to do too much, for falling prey to the secular feminist ideal of the superwoman who does it all in an effort to feel good about herself. Ironically, it's the Bible's version of a supposed Superwoman that often gets used as an example of who a Christian woman ought to be.

The Proverbs 31 woman has been invoked on both sides of the working mother conversation. Some evangelicals point out that the "work" she does is domestic in nature and therefore an example of the kind of life to which every Christian woman should aspire. However, the more convincing understanding of the "Wife of Noble Character" comes from the editors of the Quest Study Bible (and probably a few others, although the list of contributors to the Quest is basically an evangelical Who's Who, and it would be impossible to sort out who made this interpretation first), who suggest that this passage is not a biography of one ideal woman but a picture of all the options that exist for godly women.

The Quest editors note that, "this passage shows that a godly woman can find fulfillment in her home, in the community, and in a career. This passage does not limit a woman's role to any one of these areas. Nor does it create unrealistic expectations for women, calling them to do everything in all of these areas. Some women will focus more on one of these aspects than on the others. Rather than presenting an impossible dream, this epilogue to Proverbs lays out some of the possible opportunities for women who are married and have children. The wife of noble character puts wisdom into the fabric of her life."[1]

And really, isn't that what the church ought to require of us as women—that we make our decisions based on the wisdom inherent in God's leading rather than on the pressure of culture, even Christian culture? When we are allowed to listen to God, to follow the passions that God has placed in us, when we are given the tools to make wise, godly choices about our lives, it is entirely possible that God will bless and honor us with the kind of influence wielded by the Proverbs 31 ideal.

The Proverbs 31 woman provides a model of what a Christian woman can do and be when she is given permission to follow God. I look around my church and see women who are doing tremendous work for the kingdom. There are women in social services working for justice. There are women caring for children in Christian preschools. There are women who teach special needs students, women who work for the rights of children in the court system, women who raise money for charitable organizations, women who teach English to immigrants, women who mentor teenagers, and women who work with abuse victims. Imagine the gaping holes they would leave if they were told to quit these jobs because they can only be mothers. Imagine the kingdom work that would be left undone.

10

THE REAL LIFE
OF A
WORKING MOTHER

About two years ago, I wrote my editor's column about a day when all the balls I juggle—work, marriage, motherhood—started falling at the same time. I mentioned missing a deadline, having a minor fender bender that resulted in a minor "discussion" with Jim, and having my daughter's babysitter tell me that Emily seemed to need a little more "mommy time." I should have known better.

Sure enough, I got the most vitriolic letter from a reader I've ever read. A woman with a fourteen-month-old wrote to tell me that I made her sick, that I should be ashamed that the babysitter noticed something any good mother would have sensed on her own. She scolded me for working all day, coming home at 6:00 or 7:00 at night, then keeping my child up late so I could spend the time with her that I should have been giving her during the day. She told me how awful it was for women like me to be so consumed by the desire to drive a nice car (she mentioned something about a Lexus) and live in a nice house that we are willing to hand over the love and admonition of the children God gave us to complete strangers. She closed her letter by telling me to try reading what my Bible has to say about motherhood and that I ought to quit my job so a man who needed to support his family could work.

I wanted so badly to write back to this woman and tell her that I hoped her life stayed perfect, that I hoped her husband never decided to go back to school to follow his dream of being a teacher (ala Jim Barnhill) leaving her the sole breadwinner for a time. I wanted to tell her about the flexible work hours Jim and I developed so that our child was only with the babysitter three hours a day. I wanted to tell her that I went in to work early and ate lunch at my desk to make sure I could leave at 3:00. I wanted to tell her that our babysitter, Debbie, is quite possibly the most amazing woman on the planet and that even if she weren't the babysitter, I'd want Emily to spend time with her just to watch a truly godly woman in action. I wanted to send her a picture of our twelve-year-old Honda—our only car—and our modest house, which we paid for out of our hard-earned savings. I wanted to tell her God saved my sanity with a job that fits me perfectly, that it was and has continued to be so clearly where God wants me that I am constantly humbled at the privilege of doing the work I do. But I didn't.

My husband and I are cheap people. We wash our Ziploc bags, reuse aluminum foil, and only buy chicken when it's on sale for under a buck a pound.[1] We lived solely on my income when Jim was a student teacher; now that he's teaching full-time, it is entirely possible for us to live on only his salary. For now I am working, not for the money but because it's clear to me that God has a reason for putting me in this line of work.

Making Work Work

I never intended to be a working mother. I spent many post-college years agonizing about what I was going to do with my life. When I finally got my job with *Campus Life* magazine (a sister publication of *CPT*), I knew I had found an actual career.

Not only was my job professionally fulfilling, God was clearly using me in the lives of readers. I often wrote about my own experiences as a teenager and received great letters from kids telling me how something I'd written had touched them and drawn them closer to God. That was no small thing for a person who had been sinking into a deep depression over the prospect of never finding purposeful work.

I had been at my job about five months when I discovered I was pregnant with my first child. It was so obvious God had put me in my job that I couldn't imagine that having a baby would mean I'd have to leave. Jim and I talked through our options and concluded I should keep working. So we decided that (1) we would move closer to my work, (2) he would find a new job in the area as well, (3) he would ask for flexible hours at his new job, and (4) I would ask for flexible hours at mine.

It didn't take long for us to find a place to live that was two blocks from my office. It didn't take long for Jim to find a social work position with a Christian outreach organization that would let him work from noon to 8:00 p.m. It didn't take long for my boss to agree that I could work from 7:30 a.m. to 3:00 p.m. By the time Emily arrived, we had found a young woman to come to our apartment to take care of her for the three hours we needed childcare. Everything fell into place, and I kept working. We never had a sense that God was saying no to my working.

About a year after Emily was born, I moved over to *CPT*. In my position as editor, I have the privilege of helping other parents instill Christian values in their children. We get letters from readers who are struggling with challenging parenting problems; it is my honor to be part of the process of their finding help. I love knowing that the work I do actually matters to other people, and I have yet to sense God telling me to do something else.

While women such as Renee, the religion professor, and I believe God is fine with us working outside the home, this doesn't mean we don't have struggles unique to working mothers. The stress of managing multiple roles, the precarious state of maintaining childcare—if someone gets sick, the whole day can fall apart—and the exhausting effects of keeping track of hundreds of details from dental appointments to quarterly reports all take their toll on our ability to function at home or at work. These stressors affect us deeply and often bring with them heightened feelings of anxiety, depression, and worry.

What makes these feelings particularly hard to deal with is the lack of support from Christians. If a working mother complains about the stress level in her life, she's likely to be told to stop working. That's not much help for a mother who generally enjoys her work and feels God using her there. Telling her to stop working is like telling a missionary to get off the mission field when he or she complains about the heat.

Nor is it much help for a mother who needs to work to help support her family. If a man were to express frustration with the stress of his job or his struggle to find time for work and family commitments, I doubt many Christians would simply tell him to stop working. Reduce his hours? Maybe. Find a job that offered more flexibility? Perhaps. But quit and stay home with the kids? Um, no.

The Cost of Working

The life of a working mother comes with its own set of emotional issues. Most working women have little time for "extracurriculars" such as hobbies, friendships, or date nights with their hubbies. Some working mothers lose their sense of themselves because they spend so much time meeting the needs of their boss, their clients, their spouses, and their children.

Most of the working mothers I know have few close friends because mothers typically connect during the day. When I was working full-time, I had a few "mom" friends from my small group at church. But our relationships never really gelled into what I would call intimate friendships because they were home and I wasn't. They'd get together for lunch or play dates or trips to the zoo, but I couldn't go. Even when we were together, it was sometimes hard for us to relate to each other because we had spent the majority of the previous week living in completely separate spheres. I found that I often had more to talk about with their husbands, who could relate to my computer woes or my coworker troubles better than their wives could. My coworkers either didn't have children and therefore had lots of other friends, or they did have children, which meant that none of us had much time for hanging out after work.

Despite being surrounded by people for most of the day, that was a very lonely time in my life.

Then there's the spiritual fallout of being a working mother. As I said, churches often organize their women's ministries around the lives of at-home mothers, leaving mothers who work during the day few options for getting involved. But many churches also fail to provide much support for working mothers, such as affordable Christian day care or preschool, classes on being a Christian in the working world, or help with the work/family balance. There's a whole ministry organization meant to help men be successful at work and at home. Where is that kind of encouragement for working mothers?

This lack of support within the church understandably serves to remind working mothers that they are operating outside the norm, that they are living lives that, while possibly tolerated, are not necessarily sanctioned by Christians. The overt messages that many mothers get about the evils of working have an incredibly damaging impact on those mothers who work. But even the subtle message of being left on the fringes of the life of the church can leave working mothers feeling intense guilt and confusion about what they're doing and why they're doing it.

Mary Whelchel, founder of The Christian Working Woman, says, "There's a guilt that's unique to Christians. I think it's because of the attitude in some Christian circles that working mothers can't possibly be as good at parenting as their stay-at-home counterparts, and that their children can't possibly become well-adjusted adults. There are some pretty strong opinions and a lot of blame being thrown around."

The guilt that working mothers deal with is often thought of as a sign that they shouldn't be working. But Whelchel points out that there are really two kinds of guilt. She says,

Working mothers assume that every problem their children have is the result of their working. It's just not true. If you stayed home and devoted every minute to your children, they'd still have problems. You need to look closely at your emotions and determine if you're feeling true guilt or false guilt. We feel true guilt when we're not listening to God. True guilt is specific: You know why you're feeling guilty and what you're supposed to do about it. It's a matter of being obedient to God. If a mom is working and she knows God hasn't called her to that job, she better get out or she's going to be buried in guilt. If you've been putting your job ahead of your family, that's true guilt. Is your job short-changing your family? That's true guilt.

False guilt is a vague, cloudy feeling, one that's tough to nail down. It says, "I'm not right. I'm not what I should be." It feels the same and acts on you the same as true guilt, so it's tough to know the difference. But if you know you've got your priorities right and are following God's lead in your life, then you can be assured those feelings are the work of Satan, trying to find your weak spot. If it's false guilt, you need to get rid of it.[2]

Certainly we all need to be open to the voices of other Christians and be willing to hear hard truths from people we love and trust. But women, who tend to be people pleasers by nature, want to be liked, so we often let ourselves be swayed by what other people might think of us. If we get the message that we as working women are letting our children down, being selfish, or becoming obsessed with material wealth, we will start to internalize it into a kind of false guilt that doesn't come from the Holy Spirit but from our desire to be thought of as "good."

I was working full-time when Emily started preschool; a number of times I forgot to fill out a permission slip or bring snacks on my assigned day. The wonderful teachers would sometimes call with a gentle reminder to turn in the slip as soon as possible or send a kind note letting me know I could bring snacks the next week if that was more convenient for me. Even though Emily never knew I had dropped the ball, I felt guilty for not being as involved and on top of things at school as some of the other mothers. But that guilt had nothing to do with right or wrong. It had to do with my feeling as if I wasn't living up to someone else's expectations.

True guilt comes from within us and is understood by Christians to be the Holy Spirit's way of showing us where we need to make a change in our lives. Remember Traci, who telecommuted when her son was born? She felt conflicted about working and being a mother and made the choice to stop working. There was no outside pressure but rather a sensitivity to God's leading that led her to make a change. I don't know if Traci would say she felt guilty, but it's clear that God was working on her heart and that she would have eventually felt a real sense of guilt if she hadn't made her move when she felt led to.

Whether a Christian mother chooses to work or works because she has no choice, she needs the care and support of her church family. Honestly, we are so far past the point of working mothers being the exception that churches risk losing the valuable asset that working mothers—and their families—bring to the body if we don't find ways to meet their emotional and spiritual needs.

A Case Study

I got a phone call one day from a woman named Kimberly Chastain. She told me she was trying to do some research on Christian working mothers and was running into nothing but dead ends. "I thought maybe you'd have some ideas on where I should be looking," she said. I tried not to laugh.

As we talked, it was clear to both of us that Christian working mothers are so woefully underserved that it's no wonder those of us who work often feel like we're in the minority. Only a handful of books and ministry resources are available for women who want to be faithful in their work as well as their families, but Chastain is hoping to change all that.

She says, "I have been a Marriage and Family Therapist for more than fifteen years now and about two years ago added Life Coaching to my work. I wanted to specialize in a particular area as a coach. For months it seemed I couldn't get away from the idea of Christian working moms. One of the reasons I felt led to do this is I saw no books in the Christian bookstores addressing the needs of Christian working moms. I did an Internet search and found nothing. I even tried to find research data on Christian working moms and came up empty again. There seemed to be a deafening silence."

Chastain has now set up a website (www.christianworking mom.com) where she not only offers support, encouragement, and networking for working moms but also conducts a survey of working moms in an effort to create a database that can be used by the Christian community as it moves toward ministering to working mothers. So far, more than three hundred women have answered the questions about guilt, church involvement, and their spiritual formation.

Chastain's survey revealed that nearly half of the women (41 percent) felt that they had little church support as working mothers. Only 11 percent felt supported by the church; the rest said they "sometimes feel supported." At the same time, 56 percent had church responsibilities such as teaching, serving on committees, and assisting in organizing church events. Sadly, these women give their time and energy to the church but often get very little support in return. Still, ministries like Chastain's are providing a place for Christian working mothers to find the encouragement and understanding they crave.

Chastain says, "I have been amazed and blessed by the responses I've received. I have had women write from South Africa, New Zealand, Japan, Zambia, and many other countries. One woman wrote, 'Where were you several years ago when I tried to do a Bible study at my church for CWM and it caused a big problem?' A lot of women are relieved to find encouragement instead of condemnation."

11

CHRISTIAN MOTHERHOOD REVISITED

The model of motherhood perpetuated by the evangelical cult of the family has clearly led to an epidemic of emotional and spiritual fallout for many women. The model of the godly Christian mother who happily stays home with her children, who is eternally patient and giving and nurturing, who homeschools and never pops in a video so she can read the paper, whose children grow up compliant, obedient, and problem free has not only run its course, it never really had a course to begin with. There is, then, a need to replace this false model with a new understanding of motherhood, one that stands up to the way real mothers feel, the way real women live, the way real life works. Because real life is never as perfect as we'd like it to be.

Cecilia is the mother of two boys. She is a teacher, and

her husband is a youth leader. For years, they were heavily involved in ministry in their church. They were seen as up and coming leaders, core members of the church. When Cecilia was diagnosed with cancer, her church family rallied around her, providing meals, helping with the kids, extending prayer support and hospital visitations.

A few years after Cecilia went into remission, her teenage son started getting into trouble at school, was caught smoking marijuana, and seemed disinterested in church. When a friend of his committed suicide, Cecilia's son sank into a state of despondency and depression. Eventually he, too, became suicidal.

Cecilia and her husband helped him get intense therapy and admitted him to a residential treatment facility where he could regain his emotional balance and some semblance of mental health. This tragic situation, one that Cecilia would say took an even greater toll on her family than her cancer, went unnoticed by her church. There were few meals, few offers of help and support, few people asking how they were holding up.

Cecilia found that the church seemed unable to minister to the emotional crisis in her family. She says, "Not one of the pastors came to really talk to us. The church provided funds to help with our son's hospitalization but very little emotional or spiritual support. There was an attitude that our son's mental illness was the result of his sin. We were told that if he would just turn to God and ask for forgiveness, everything would be okay. The son of one of our pastors had tried to commit suicide and it was understood that he had an illness. But when our son tried to kill himself, we were told that he was just a kid trying to escape the consequences of his mistakes." Cecilia and her husband were questioned about their parenting style: Perhaps they'd been too lax with their son. Maybe they hadn't emphasized Scripture strongly enough. This church needed to place blame in order to preserve the idea that good parenting can prevent this kind of tragedy.

When families like Cecilia's get the spiritual shaft because their lives don't turn out the way they hoped, there is a ripple effect in the whole church. After their experience, Cecilia's family left the church they'd attended for years to find a place where they could be open about the tremendous suffering in their lives. They also wanted their sick son to have a faith community where he would find hope and healing, not judgment. Their former church lost a family of committed, gifted people simply because it couldn't make room for a family in pain.

The Practice of Mothering

I spent last Friday night at a memorial service for three little boys, a set of triplets born at twenty weeks gestation and alive for only an hour. The boys' bodies had been cremated, and their parents carried the boys' ashes in three tiny enamel jars. Early in the service, these heartbroken parents set the jars on the altar, then took their seats in the front pew. But a few minutes later the mother stood up, walked to the altar, grabbed the three jars, and went back to her seat. Every other mother in the room understood why. She needed to hold her babies.

Motherhood isn't about the work involved in raising children. It isn't a set of tasks or expectations. My friend would never take her sons to the playground or help them with their homework, but she is a mother. She would never read them a Bible story or monitor their television viewing, but she is a Christian mother. She claims that name not because of the work she did, but because her heart has been filled with love for her three little boys, and she will never be the same.

In some ways, it's impossible to create a model of motherhood. Mothering, after all, is a relationship, not a job, and relationships never fall into neat categories. So rather than present a vision of motherhood that does little more than rewrite the job description a bit, I'd like to suggest that we stop thinking of motherhood as something we do, or even as something we are, and instead envision motherhood as a practice through which we ourselves are formed.

Philosopher Alasdair MacIntyre introduced the idea of practices as the framework for a system of ethics and moral philosophy in his book *After Virtue.* His basic premise is that living an ethical life involves acquiring a particular kind of character or set of virtues. We acquire virtue through certain practices—activities we participate in that have a standard of excellence, and through which we have a positive impact on the larger community.[1]

We participate in all kinds of practices that form us, even if we're not always aware of them. Playing the piano, taking pictures, making soup—these are practices that shape us. In order to do them well, we have to do them over and over, getting better at them each time. As we do them, we develop certain virtues that are necessary for doing the practice well. Learning an instrument takes perseverance and commitment. Photography involves discernment and creativity. Cooking demands patience and attentiveness. While you can develop perseverance through other practices, you can't become an excellent piano player without it. There is, then, a cycle of virtues and practices. As we participate in the practices, we develop the virtues necessary to continue that participation.

The practices of faith work the same way. We believe that prayer, service, discipleship, meditation, fellowship, and worship are essential to our spiritual development because we recognize that as we do these things, we discover more about life with God. As we experience God at work in us, we find our faith growing deeper. And as our faith grows deeper, we seek out new ways to experience God at work in us.

The practice of motherhood starts even before our children are born. Pregnant women give up drinking Diet Coke or using Advil in order to protect their unborn children, acts that take self-control and sacrificial love. Women who go through the years-long process of adopting a child develop extraordinary patience. If a child has special needs, that mother will have to have virtues such as compassion and resiliency. It takes selflessness to wake up every three hours for months on end to feed a hungry newborn. It takes patience to dress a toddler. It takes humility to apologize when you've lost your temper with a five-year-old. The more we use the virtues necessary to be good mothers, the more those virtues become part of our character. And what is the Christian life if not an ongoing process of striving to develop the character of Christ?

The truth is, mothering changes us. I used to think of myself as a loving person, but I have never experienced the kind of fierce, protective, intense love I feel for Emily and Isaac. Despite my pacifist leanings, I would gladly take on anyone who even thought of harming them (and win, I might add). One of the women I surveyed said, "Motherhood has been an awakening personally, spiritually, emotionally, and physically to grow into the person God wants me to be." Another woman in my survey said, "Being a mom has driven me to be more of the person God wants me to be by exposing my weaknesses such as a lack of self-control or love or forgiveness or wisdom." Still another said, "At times, being a parent brings out the worst traits in me, traits that need refinement and weren't revealed before I had children." When we think of mothering as a practice through which we are formed by God, suddenly, the ups and downs of motherhood fit into a context of God's intentions for *our* lives.

For us to reframe motherhood as a practice, we have to get rid of some basic evangelical assumptions about motherhood, namely that it's solely about raising godly kids. We need to recognize that God uses parenting to form us, to shape *our* character, to move us toward being more like Christ. Our relationships with our children change us indelibly. Certainly we are an important factor in their spiritual formation, but they are just as important in ours.

We also need to let go of the notion that the results of our parenting—i.e., perfect children—are the best test of our success as mothers. If that were true, God would be a failure as a parent. I mean, look at the state of God's children! Of course, we understand that (1) it is our sinful nature, not God's parenting, that leads us down destructive paths and (2) our relationship with God is based on far more than our ability to be obedient and follow God's commands. Yet we think of human parenting in "if/then" terms—if I do everything right, then my kids will turn out okay.

Once these assumptions are put away, we can more easily get our heads around the idea of motherhood as one of the ways God grows us as people. If I do say so myself, the concept of the practice of motherhood makes a whole lot more sense than thinking of it as a job, a role, a calling, or any other kind of stagnant entity. A mother's relationship with her children is beyond comprehension. It is filled with

150

mystery and wonder and richness. It is a reflection of the two complex and wonderful creations who make up the relationship. It is *never* stagnant. The late Dennis Guernsey once wrote, "People in their significant relationships are moving, creating, active beings. Life can't be represented as an organizational chart. Adaptation and flexibility are as important as structure and permanence."[2]

The church has focused on the work of motherhood rather than the relationship between a mother and her children, which in turn prevents women from truly releasing themselves to the profound depth of their connection to their children. Thinking of motherhood in terms of relationships in process, rather than results, is much more in keeping with the heart of the gospel, which, according to Jesus, is all about relationships: God's relationship with us ("Love the Lord your God with all your heart and with all your soul and with all your mind"), and our relationship with others ("Love your neighbor as yourself" Luke 10:27).

I truly believe that the cult of the family grew, in part, out of a desire to give mothers a sense that their work in raising children mattered, that they had been given a holy and noble calling. But that intent gradually went awry, stripping the beauty and holiness out of motherhood and replacing it with false expectations and a fear of failure. If we want to reclaim motherhood as something worth pouring ourselves into, something that is touched by God, we have to have a theology of motherhood in which God is still present in the life of the mother.

Motherhood and the Bible

The new theology of motherhood I'm proposing will also demand a major shift in the way many churches think about women in general. Sadly, far too many evangelical communities still view women as second-class Christians, not fully capable or called to participate in the life of the church. If the church believes that motherhood, that family, is an essential part of who we are as Christians, we need to move mothers in particular and women in general back to a place of equal footing with men. If the church believes that its purpose is to develop disciples, it needs to take the discipleship of women seriously. It simply must become a place where our faith is allowed to thrive, where we are given not just permission but *invitations* to use our gifts, to explore what it means for us to be daughters of the King, to walk in the way of Jesus in whatever capacity God leads us.

We can't get to this point without stripping away our ideas of what we *think* the Bible says about women. For some evangelicals, the idea of feminist theology—which they would define as any theology that speaks of equality between men and women—reeks of modern, secular culture. In reality, though, the idea that men and women bear the image of God in equal doses and are therefore equal participants in the kingdom of God is as ancient as creation itself.

Theologian Gilbert Bilezikian makes the argument that the Bible really needs to be understood in three stages: creation, the fall, and redemption in the form of the old and new covenants. He says,

> *Creation* refers to the divine initiative that resulted in establishing the cosmos and, within it, a privileged environment that would provide a context for human life. . . .
>
> The *fall* refers to the temporary thwarting of divine purposes that resulted from human mutiny against God's will. The fall created multiple disruptions in the original design of creation. Those disruptions affected all aspects

of human life and of the environment without destroying them completely. . . .

The word *redemption* points to that aspect of God's nature that refuses to abandon fallen humans to the consequences of their rebellion. . . . God's activity in relation to Abraham and his descendants is properly called the "old covenant" since its purpose was to set the stage for a fulfillment that it could only anticipate in faith and foreshadow in its institutions. . . .

[The intent of the "new covenant"] was to restore the original purposes of creation through the ministry of Jesus Christ and in the new community that He established, the church.[3]

So basically, everything we believe about how God created the world has to be based on the first two chapters of Genesis, before the fall. Once sin enters and creation as God intended it has fallen apart, the rest of the Old Testament is a reflection of a fallen world and God's efforts to repair it. It's not until Jesus arrives that humanity is restored to a right relationship with God, and even then, the final restoration will not be complete until the second coming of Christ.

The only way to free women to experience their lives as God intended is to better understand what that intention was. And there is nothing in the Genesis account to suggest that God intended for women to play a supporting role in the world. J. Lee Grady points out that not only is it a mistaken reading of Genesis to say women are inferior to men but one could argue that, since every act of creation bested the one before it (earth, then plants, then animals, then a human being), Eve is actually the crowning achievement of God's creation.[4]

Bilezikian explains there is no evidence in the creation narrative to suggest that Eve/woman is anything other than Adam/man's equal partner in creation. He says, "The teachings of the second chapter of Genesis . . . provide a rationale for the essential unity of human nature in male and female. They also show that in God's creation ideal, man and woman were expected to enjoy a relationship of mutuality in equality."[5]

Mary Stewart Van Leeuwen points out, "Not only are both male and female created in God's image as social beings, but both are given dominion over the rest of creation. Some Christians who argue for stereotypical gender roles . . . have actually argued for male headship on the basis of Genesis 1:26, stating that it gives dominion to Adam. Either they have not read the rest of the chapter or they are deliberately ignoring it. . . . Both the man and woman are told to fill the earth and subdue it; both are told to be fruitful and multiply; both are told they have dominion over every other living thing."[6] Frankly, a woman can't fulfill this God-given command if the range of her dominion is limited to her immediate family.

The only way for motherhood to be understood as a practice of spiritual formation is to free women from the idea that our femaleness prevents us from exploring all God has to offer us as children of God. In her book *A Potent Spell,* psychotherapist Janna Malamud Smith says, "What a child needs most is a free mother, one who feels that she is in fact living *her* life, and has adequate food, sleep, wages, education, safety, opportunity, institutional support, child care, and loving relationships. 'Adequate' means enough to allow her to participate in the world—and in mothering—without starving, or feeling economically trapped or uncompensated, continually exploited, terrorized, devalued, battered, chronically exhausted, or virtually enslaved."[7] If we really want children to thrive, families to be places where

God is alive, and women to live the lives God created them for, we have to give mothers this kind of freedom.

A New Theology at Work

Understanding motherhood as a practice gives us a way of overcoming the tripping points of the current evangelical model of motherhood. When we view motherhood as a process through which God shapes us, we are able to let go of the idea that the results of our parenting are all that matter. Instead, our focus turns to the ways in which God is at work in our mothering. We know that God will use our mistakes, our missteps, our failures to turn us into someone more like Jesus.

We also escape the cult of the family trap when we recognize that motherhood is *a* practice of faith but not *the* practice of faith. God is alive and busy in the lives of my single friends, my childless friends, my working-mom friends, and my stay-at-home mom friends. Who are we to suggest that God's work in the lives of those who have children is somehow more formative than his work in the life of infertile or unmarried women?

The formation that happens in the practice of mothering does more than make us better mothers. As we grow more compassionate, more patient, more gentle, more humble as mothers, we carry those virtues into other parts of our lives and into other practices. I've found that being a mother has made me much more tenderhearted. When I see a news report about some criminal, part of me remembers that he is not a monster but rather someone's little boy who was deeply damaged by the people and experiences in his life. This tenderness carries over into my marriage, my relationship with my parents, my friendships, and my job.

Most importantly, a theology of motherhood as a practice puts mothering clearly in the context of the gospel. Rather than family being the ultimate expression of a woman's worth, it can be a place in which her authentic self, the person she is in God, is refined and reformed. Family moves from being an end in itself to being a means to an even greater end—the bringing about of the kingdom of God.

Bilezikian says, "The transforming power of the gospel needs to be applied to individual lives *and* to the way Christians relate among themselves. . . . Nowhere does the Scripture command us to develop our sex-role awareness as males or females. It calls us—both men and women—to aquire the mind of Christ and to be transformed in His image (Gal. 3:27; Eph. 4:13; Phil. 2:5; and so on). Both men and women are called to develop their 'inner man,' which means their basic personhood in cooperation with the Holy Spirit."[8]

Indeed, the apostle Paul says that in Christ, there is no male nor female (Gal. 3:28). Life in Christ frees us from the arbitrary expectations of culture and moves us into lives where God is at work in all that we are and all that we do. When motherhood is a practice through which God works on a woman's spirit, it goes from being a role filled with high expectations and the resultant disappointments to being a holy relationship touched and covered by the love and grace of God.

A Case Study

If you want to know what the practice of motherhood really looks like, spend a day or two with the adoptive parents of special needs children. My friend Camille has four kids—two are biologically hers, and two were adopted after being removed from their abusive home and spending several years in foster care. Camille told me, "I dreaded the thought of these two children being parented by people who didn't know how much they needed to be part of a family where the husband loves and supports his wife instead of hitting her until the police have to intervene, a family where a mother will love and nurture them and choose them over an addiction to drugs and alcohol."

When Camille and her family adopted these two children, they knew they were in for a difficult road. Sure enough, the older boy has been violent at school and at home, and his younger sister has been abusive and combative with her adoptive family. Camille says, "I'm grateful I didn't have a clue how very hard it would be."

My friend Tandy and her family adopted a daughter from an overseas orphanage. She says, "There have been tremendous challenges, but the rewards have been awesome. I have learned that God is capable of providing wisdom as we parent our children through situations we never imagined we'd be dealing with. If someone would have told me I'd have to know how to handle a child as she grieved her biological family, I would have wondered if I was capable, but God provided me with wisdom and gave me insight to help Rayna through this time. I've seen God heal the emotional and physical damage that occurred in Rayna's past. I can see that God can work through my weaknesses to bond our whole family together."

Camille says, "I am very aware that I do not possess the ability to parent these kids on my own. I have been an eyewitness to what God is doing in our family. God shows up when I have to do a physical safety hold on my eight-year-old who has just called me horrible, vulgar names and spit yogurt all over my face. I can hold her for an hour while she spews out all of her pain, anger, frustration, and abandonment all over me. It's not me holding her, it's God holding both of us."

Adoption, particularly the adoption of older children or those with special needs, has nothing to do with being a perfect parent. It isn't for those who believe that good parenting can overcome a history of abuse. It is about knowing that there are thousands and thousands of children in the world who are hungry and hurting and in desperate need of compassion. It's about recognizing that when Jesus told us to care for widows and orphans (James 1:27), he meant it.

In adopting these children, Camille and Tandy have taken a tremendous risk. They went into adoption knowing they were opening themselves up to unimaginable challenges. As they parent these children, Camille and Tandy recognize that how their children "turn out" is only a small part of what God is doing in their families. They recognize that they are being formed in amazing ways, that they are being obedient to God's call on the lives of God's people. Camille says, "I do this because I know this is right. If I continue to open my heart, home, and pocketbook to these children, I am following God."

12

PRACTICING MOTHERHOOD

The idea that motherhood is a practice certainly makes for great theory, but unless we can get our heads around what it means to our daily lives as moms, it won't do us much good. Still, this is the tricky part. Alasdair MacIntyre's definition of a practice includes the criterion that an activity can only be a practice if it has "standards of excellence which are appropriate to, and partially definitive of, that form of activity."[1] For something to be considered a practice, we have to be able to say that it's possible to be good at it. (That's why an activity like tossing a football in the backyard isn't a practice; you don't have to be good at it to do it. As long as the ball successfully reaches the other person most of the time, you're okay. The *game* of football is another story; you have to understand the rules and have some level of skill to play the game of football. You can't just run around a field with a ball and call it football.) On the surface, it sounds as if we're headed back to "the-proof-is-in-the-pudding" parenting, but if we dig a littler deeper, it's clear that the practice of motherhood is a whole new ball game.

Admittedly, excellence in motherhood *is* partly about meeting some basic criteria, such as providing food and shelter, which is why the Florida woman who left her toddler alone in her apartment for three weeks is not, at present, a good mother. But we all know of horrible mothers who have raised wonderful children and vice versa. The standards of excellence, then, have nothing to do with how our children turn out and everything to do with how we approach mothering.

When we understand motherhood as a practice of spiritual formation, the rules of the game, as it were, change dramatically. What matters in the practice of mothering is our willingness to be open to God's work in our lives, our ability to grow and change with our children, our vulnerability and honesty in the face of the challenges that every brand of spiritual development present. Just as our criteria for determining what makes for excellent worship or prayer are less about the forms and more about the attitude, so, too, is the practice of mothering marked by our capacity to allow God to enter into our lives and do what needs to be done in our hearts and minds. When we strive for excellence in these areas, the problems presented by the current evangelical model of the perfect Christian mother fade away.

Moving out of Depression

Depression, as you'll recall, can grow out of all kinds of circumstances, including an unresolved sense of loss. For Christian women, that loss is often the result of life not looking like we'd expected it to—we aren't the wonderful mothers we thought we'd be (or perhaps not mothers at all), our children are not who we hoped they'd be, and our days feel dull and pointless rather than fulfilling. Because these feelings are not talked about in the church, we assume no one else feels the way we do, which then adds to the cycle of failure and depression that affects so many women.

The practice of motherhood can move women out of the spiral of depression in a number of ways. Primarily, when motherhood is seen as a practice of spiritual formation, the only way to fail is to close ourselves off to God's work in our lives. To shut God out, to ignore the instincts God has placed in us, to follow the crowd—even the Christian crowd—without discernment, these are the signs of failure, not a sassy daughter or a suicidal son. I would go so far as to say that the only real failure in mothering comes when a woman believes she has motherhood all figured out and becomes resistant to change.

As the practice of motherhood strips away our evangelical expectations, women find the freedom to enjoy motherhood without the fear of failure. Claire, one of the moms I surveyed, said, "I have gotten over being interested in what others think of my parenting. We do what works great for us, and I have this loving child who tells me I'm a good mommy. I don't want to not listen to myself just because other people are doing it differently. Only I know my particular child and what's best for her." This mom is invested in the process of building a relationship with her child. She has learned to pay attention to her instincts and the needs of her unique child. She has found freedom, not fear, in mothering. She has met a standard of excellence.

Cameron Lee, Professor of Family Studies at Fuller Theological Seminary, says our goal as mothers ought to be becoming "good-enough parents."[2] What he means is that rather than investing so much worry into trying to be perfect—an unattainable goal—we should instead give ourselves the grace God gives us and let our mistakes as parents inform us and shape us as invaluable steps in the journey of becoming more Christlike. When our view shifts to "good-enough" parenting, we are less likely to fall into the spiral of dashed expectations, intense frustration, and anxiety that can so often lead to depression.

I'm certainly not suggesting that depression is just a state of mind—there are serious physiological reasons people suffer from depression. However, I do believe that for many mothers, depression is also the result of the near-constant message that we are failing at "the most important job in the world." We can take a giant step toward helping women deal with these feelings by thinking of motherhood as a practice of spiritual formation, where even our failings can be used by God to create something wonderful.

Discovering the World Outside

Another mark of an excellent mother is her willingness to move beyond the walls of her family home and find ways to participate in other kingdom practices in order to fulfill Christ's call on all Christians to go out and make disciples. My biggest beef with the cult of the family is how strongly it pulls us away from our real calling as Christians—to bring God's love, grace, and mercy to all the world. By creating a kind of tunnel vision where all that really matters is the nuclear family, the church has turned our heads from all the other ways in which God can and will use us in the world.

It makes some Christians nervous to suggest that the family isn't the most important entity in God's kingdom. The family is certainly a beautiful institution and God undoubtedly uses our family relationships to form us, but from a biblical perspective, there is no evidence that the family is the only stage upon which God acts. The truth is that the Bible doesn't say much about being a good mother. Sure, there are a few passages here and there that specifically speak about motherhood or parenting. There is a running theme of passing our faith on to future generations—an idea that is as much about building the Christian community as it is about the family. But those passages are never the crux of a chapter or the main thrust of a letter from Paul or of one of Jesus' parables.

As I've said, it could be argued that the family often gets in the way of people doing God's work in the world. Jesus told his followers it was entirely possible that they would have to turn against their families to follow him (Luke 12:52–53). The apostle Paul told his audiences it was better for them to remain single than to let family commitments prevent them from serving God (1 Cor. 7:32–35).

We have to allow for the possibility that it's not only okay with God if we open ourselves up to being used in non-maternal ways, but that it can actually be a really good thing. Because motherhood is a practice of spiritual formation, rather than the sum total of who we are as women with children, there is room for us to participate in other practices as well—friendships, work, community service, ministry. Erin says, "I think motherhood is a highly valuable and godly occupation, but I don't think it's the only way God will use women. As a mother of three boys, I have worked hard at parenting but have always tried to keep growing in my walk with God, keeping open to how he would use me in the kingdom in other ways. As we approach the empty nest, I feel prepared to continue the work God has done in me as Erin, not Erin the mother."

The practice of motherhood requires us to establish a sense of who we are as children of God, to remember that God has work to do in us that may or may not take place in the context of mothering. That doesn't necessarily mean that we all need to head to an overseas mission field—although we ought to be open to the idea. But it does mean that it's legitimate for us to have needs that aren't met in motherhood. Just as it's dangerous for a woman to assume that a husband will fulfill all of her emotional needs, it's not healthy to assume that motherhood will "complete" us, if you will.

Becoming open to the other practices through which God can form us takes a little bit of psychological work. We have to get in tune with the passions God has placed in us. A lot of women find it helpful to journal, but I find it even more helpful to read my old journals from the pre-kid days when I did a lot more navel gazing. When I read about the hopes and dreams of my twenty-five-year-old self, I'm reminded that many of those desires are still there, that I still want to have an impact on the world. Even without an old journal, it's essential for us to return to the passionate girls we were, to the idealistic dreams we had about who God created us to be and how God might use us to build the kingdom. God put those desires there for a reason, and we need to trust that God is big enough to both use us outside of our families and keep our families intact.

My friend Anna has found that motherhood has actually helped her discover new passions. She says, "Having children and staying home with them has opened up a more artistic side of my personality that I think I always lacked the self-confidence to explore. I've always loved taking pictures, but it never occurred to me that it could be a career choice. Now it seems like something I can pursue along with being a stay-at-home mom. It's something that really excites me."

As mothers, we have an intense desire to make the world better for our children. But imagine what mothers could do if we put that same intensity into building the kingdom of God. We would be following in the path of the Christian mothers who were integral to the abolition of slavery, the development of the women's temperance movement, and reforms in child labor laws. Virtues such as compassion, kindness, creativity, and humility that are refined in the practice of motherhood can and should be used in other arenas to bring God's love, peace, mercy, and justice to the world.

When we recognize motherhood as a practice, we can make room for other practices that shape our Christlike character, which in turn makes us better mothers. The virtues I need to be a good editor—patience, attentiveness, persistence—flow back into my mothering. The same is true of the virtues it takes for us to be good daughters, good friends, good wives. When a woman changes the diaper of her elderly mother, she is being formed. When a woman manages a conflict with a coworker, she is being formed. When a woman makes her husband's favorite meal even though she's had an exhausting day, she is being formed. All the practices we participate in shape us, and God can use them all to help us become the people we are meant to be.

Mothering Our Way

A few years ago, a book came out that promoted feeding babies on a schedule, rather than on demand. I talked with one father who, along with his wife, had used this method on their son. He proudly told me, "Our baby was sleeping through the night at four weeks!" I know enough about babies to know that most newborns need to eat every two to three hours for the first eight weeks or so, particularly breastfed babies. It seemed to me that this triumph of sleep over eating—not to mention the parents' desire for control winning out over the baby's desire for a full tummy—was less about what was good for the baby and more about what was good for the parents. Sadly, a lot of Christian parenting advice strikes me the same way.

While much of what is written about Christian parenting is gilded in a coating of "this is what's best for your children," it still seems clear to me that the emphasis on obedience (teach your children to obey so they will know how to obey God), authoritarian discipline (children need to behave in order to learn respect for God's rules), and parental control (you are the parent, so what you say goes) is not really about children at all.

A friend told me about his sister who spanked her eleven-month-old for climbing the stairs. The sister has read lots of Christian books that teach her that she needs to establish authority over her daughter early on or the child will act out in more dangerous and inappropriate ways as she gets older. On the surface this advice is about the safety and emotional development of the child, but a closer look reveals that it's really about making sure the child knows who's the boss and molding her into a compliant child who does what she's told. And so this mom is spanking a baby who any child development expert would say is not old enough to make a conscious choice to disobey her mother.

My daughter is a feisty six-year-old, and I often find myself getting frustrated when she throws a fit because her brother has taken a toy or when she has a hard time sharing with a friend. But really, I'm not so much frustrated by what she's doing as I am by the mere fact that now I have to stop what I'm doing and deal with a situation. I get annoyed because I am inconvenienced. Sometimes I find that I'm irritated simply because I think I should have raised a child who doesn't do those things.

Life would certainly be easier if Emily was a compliant child, but that's not how God made her. Instead, she is a strong-willed, funny, enthusiastic, imaginative, spirited little girl whom I wouldn't trade for anything. I fully believe that my job as her mother is not to squelch what God has placed in her but to nurture it and help her discover how to use all her amazing gifts in the world. I often operate in full squelch mode, but in my heart I know that God has fitted my daughter with a very special set of gifts, and he has plans for those gifts I can't even begin to imagine.

Excellence in the practice of motherhood is also found in our ability to recognize what is unique in our children and to parent them accordingly. When we allow the cult of the family to dictate how we parent our children, the kinds of discipline we should use, and what schooling is best for them, we are forced to strip away what is special about them, those leaves and blossoms that sometimes grow where we'd prefer them not to. But it is often those buds that are most God-inspired in our children. The very aspects of Emily's personality that sometimes make her hard to parent are the things that make her a delightful kid. They are the things that will make her an incredible woman of God one day. As the old saying goes, "God doesn't make mistakes." God created Emily exactly as she should be, and I do her a great disservice if I spend my time and energy trying to turn her into someone else.

The practice of mothering allows us to break out of the mind-set that we have to somehow turn our children into perfect adults, rather than nurture the people God created them to be—after all, if we are still in the process of formation, surely our children are as well. The difference is that the practice of motherhood takes away the fear of messing up our kids. Because we place our trust in God's work both in our lives and in the lives of our children, we can let go of the idea that if we use time-outs instead of spanking or if we send our kids to public school we will have done them irreparable harm.

We can also let go of our fear that something bad will happen to our children. Because of our access to media we know way too much about what kinds of dangers are out there. We are therefore willing to do whatever it takes to keep our children from physical, emotional, and spiritual harm. Janna Malamud Smith says, "Becoming a mother, one finds oneself living in a mental state that moves between quiet vigilance and high alert—even the luckiest among us, even in our ahistorical sheltered safety. The maternal mind is a sheepdog herding a flock in the rain—nudging, circling, barking, nipping heels, keeping an eye out for predators, and panting with effort that may or may not accomplish its aim. We sense that somewhere, maybe close or maybe not, wolves threaten. We labor to keep them away."[3]

Whether consciously or unconsciously, the church has capitalized on mothers' instinctive need to protect our children. So we read the articles and sign up for the seminars that promise the key to good parenting, which is, in turn, the key to keeping our children from harm. But when we read the Bible, we see that there's no such thing as a safe life, even for God's most obedient servants. We can obey God all day long and still meet with great suffering and sorrow.

In truth, we cannot protect our children from the pains of life. What we can do is help them develop the kind of faith that carries them through the heartaches and struggles they're likely to find as they move through the world. Doing so means letting go of our need to control our children or get them to walk down a prescribed path. It means recognizing that God has crafted each child with hopes and dreams of her own, with a personality and set of passions that we are to tend, not tame.

Surviving at Home

Julie is the mother of two preschoolers who are nineteen months apart. She spent more than three years either pregnant or nursing. She told me, "When I stopped nursing my youngest child, I felt this sense of liberation!" Julie loves being home. She loves being a mom. But as she looked at her life after the fog of the baby and toddler days began to lift, she noticed that she had needs that weren't being met through her mothering. "I made a list of what I need to feel balanced in my life, and the two things missing were time for myself and exercise." And so Julie is considering taking a job delivering newspapers in the early morning hours. "I love the early morning, and I love the idea of being by myself for two hours in the quiet." On top of that, she and her husband, a pastor at a small church, would love to have a little more money, and the paper route would be an easy way for Julie to make a small income. Sounds like a no-brainer, doesn't it?

After teasing Julie about being a mom with a paper route, riding her bike and tossing papers on people's roofs, I asked her why she didn't take a retail job or a coffee-shop job where she could get out of the house, make some cash, and not have to wake up at 4:00 a.m. She said, "I have to balance what I need—time to myself—with the stress it would bring to me and to our family." For Julie, adding another social demand—dealing with coworkers and customers—and juggling schedules with her husband is adding stress, not balance.

Julie is a smart mom for two reasons (well, more than two, but for my purposes, we'll stick with two): she knows what she needs, and she knows how to seek balance. For stay-at-home moms, these are crucial elements of practicing motherhood with excellence.

The last thing I want to do is to send stay-at-home moms into a frenzy of trying to find out what else they can do to fill their days. But Julie is onto something with her list of what she needs to be a balanced, healthy person. That's an exercise every mother could benefit from, particularly stay-at-home moms, who typically give little thought to their own needs.

Some women might find that their needs are being met, that they have found the balance that works for them. My friend Claire says, "I will not give up my own self. I have a book club, a moms' night out, and dates with my husband. I want my daughter to see that even though I'm home with her, I still have to take care of myself in order to be a good mother." Other mothers might discover areas of need they never put words to before, such as the need for a deep friendship or the need for more time with God or time to volunteer in the community.

Once we're honest about our needs, we can take steps to meet those needs in healthy ways. That starts with knowing ourselves and our gifts, and knowing our limits. Then we need to listen to God and allow ourselves to be led through the doors God opens for us. I know this isn't the right time in my life to jump into community theater, but I have a very small part in our church Christmas play and that's enough for now. My friend Sue is heavily involved in the Mothers' Fellowship at her church and finds tremendous fulfillment in ministering to other mothers. My friend Debbie took a spiritual gifts class at her church and felt she had a real passion for children. So she started caring for three young children in her home, a ministry that also allows her to homeschool her two children. Because the practice of motherhood invites us to focus on what God is doing in us, we can be open to the other practices that flow together with our motherhood to help us become whole, healthy women who seek God in all that we do.

Practicing at Work

Clearly, when we understand motherhood as a practice, there is more than enough room for mothers to work outside the home, for there is formative value in work as well as in mothering. A willingness to enter into what God is doing in the world is also a mark of excellence in motherhood.

A few weeks ago in church, our pastor talked about the idea of our vocation being a way in which we join in the work God is doing in the world. During our post-sermon discussion time, one man admitted that he couldn't see how his job as a data entry clerk for an insurance company was part of God's work. Doug, the pastor, offered an explanation that was nothing short of brilliant—that by helping people get compensated for their health care, this clerk was involved in the work of justice and mercy and compassion. And he thought he just filled out forms!

Those of us who are working mothers know that we acquire all kinds of virtues in the work we do. We are shaped when we have to patiently deal with irate customers or tenderly change the dressing on a patient's wound. We are shaped when we calmly react to a student's tantrum or a boss's tirade. We are shaped by the sheer mental work it takes to be fully present at work and at home. This shaping is an essential part of our formation as people of God.

Being working mothers who are striving to meet the standards of excellence still means making a careful evaluation of the work we do outside of the home and our reasons for doing it (a process that wouldn't hurt stay-at-home moms or working dads, for that matter). Women who are truly working only for the money need to ask difficult questions of themselves and their families: Could we survive without my income? Are there ways we could cut down on our expenses? Is the stress of my working worth the income my job is bringing in? How can my husband and I work together to create the kind of family life that nurtures all of us?

Women (and men) who work outside the home also need to determine where their work fits into the work of God.[4] This goes beyond the notion that we are salt and light to our non-Christian coworkers, although that is certainly a worthy result of working and expands to include this idea that the work we do forms us. If we are going to sacrifice time with our children—and believe me, I would never claim that working outside the home doesn't demand sacrifice—then we need to make sure we are doing so for a greater purpose, one that is part of bringing about the love, mercy, justice, peace, and hope that are the hallmarks of the kingdom of God. When we seek God in our work, the jobs we hold outside our homes, away from our families, contribute to God's work in the world. And that is the calling of every Christian.

13

THE NEW MODEL
FOR CHURCHES

The messages the church sends about motherhood have had an enormous impact on the way mothers think about themselves. Most of the women I surveyed said that their ideas about who and what a mother should be were shaped by the women they watched in church when they were growing up, by the messages in Christian books and pulpits about a woman's place, and by the unspoken pressure to fit into a particular mold of mothering. So it follows that women will have a very difficult time thinking of motherhood as a practice unless the church reframes its approach to motherhood as well.

Every Christian community will need to forge its own path toward a new perspective on motherhood; what works for a small church in Minneapolis might not work for a mega-church in California. But I am convinced that each Christian community owes it to its women to rethink the way it ministers to this underserved part of the body. If we are going to return motherhood to a place where it is honored and supported by the church, where it is thought of with respect rather than idolatry, we have to commit to exploring new ideas for nurturing the spiritual formation of all women.

There are plenty of bright spots in the evangelical culture (and lots of bright spots outside of it that are worth looking at as well) that can guide the church as we seek out fresh means of ministering to women. They offer a set of principles that can serve as an excellent starting place for reforming the church's view of motherhood.

All Women Are Equal

When we first moved to Minneapolis, I was invited to join a few other moms with young children for a play group. I went once, and that was enough for me. Maybe it's because I deal with parenting issues for a living. Maybe it's because my daughter was five at the time and all the other kids were toddlers. Maybe it's because my depression was still undiagnosed and I just didn't have the emotional energy to invest myself in new friendships. Whatever the reason, I didn't click with the other women in the group. All we had in common was the fact that we had children, and frankly, I need more than that.

About a year ago, a woman at my church started planning "Women's Events." Our church is only a few years old and is a grassroots kind of place, so formally organized events are pretty rare. But this woman set aside a time and invited all the women from the church to an evening of dessert and conversation. That was it: food and talking. There was no speaker, no agenda, no plan. More importantly, there was no "target audience"; every woman was invited. The night of the event, I sat at a small table with two single women in their twenties, a single mom in her thirties, and two sisters in their fifties with adult children. We had a blast. On the surface, we had very little in common, but that's what made our conversation so valuable. We talked about work and clothes and friends and how hard it is to get to know people and raising children and divorce and just about everything else. I left the event feeling as if I'd made real friends.

Most women are social creatures. We need each other deeply, and we crave opportunities to connect on an intimate level with other women; but we are also complex people with all kinds of interests. When we are corralled with other mothers or other singles or other newly marrieds, we can certainly find things to talk about, but our view is rarely expanded. It's only moderately helpful for me to talk about potty training with another mother of a toddler. I get more out of hearing a grandmother tell me that she couldn't have survived raising her four preschoolers without the help of her teenaged sister. Her experience gives me a long view of motherhood, something that, for me, is more valuable than advice about training a two-year-old.

I have also found it invaluable to have friends who don't have children at all. My childless friends have been a kind of salvation for me as I've dealt with my depression. I love talking with them about work and men and parents and all kinds of other issues that have nothing to do with my children. They have helped me start figuring out who I am when I'm not pretending to have my act together. I think that we mothers surrender large chunks of our brains to the care of our kids (all those schedules have to go somewhere), and my single friends have reminded me that I have lots of brain left over for other conversations as well.

Perhaps the most effective ministry to mothers churches can have is to give them access to ministries that have nothing to do with mothering. I am a big fan of MOPS, and I'll talk more about them in a minute, but every church with a MOPS ministry, or any other kind of group for mothers, needs to make sure they are offering a variety of times and places for *all* women to gather and connect: book clubs, outreach opportunities, knitting clubs, Bible studies, art classes, yoga, and the list goes on. Not only are such opportunities essential for the spiritual health of women with children, they are essential to women, period.

The Family of God Comes First

The only way for the church to truly be pro-family is by enabling all families to live the lives God leads them toward. That means helping working mothers find safe, affordable childcare. (It might even mean starting a day-care center so we can *be* that safe, affordable childcare.) It means offering respite care and support for foster families, adoptive families, or any family that's struggling to survive. It means recognizing that the families who sit in our sanctuaries are made up of stepfamilies, single parents, working mothers, adopted children, and kids with developmental and behavioral problems and adjusting our ministry options accordingly. These things don't have to come out of formal programs or committees. All that's needed is an openness to the realities of life and a willingness to walk together in the journey toward God.

We have a woman at our church whose husband is in jail; she has four young children and is barely eking out a living. It's been beautiful to see the ways in which our community has stepped into her life to give her the strength to survive and even thrive. It's been beautiful to see her accept the help she knows she needs. We're not trying to change her situation as much as support her so she can find ways to change it herself. We have several social service professionals at our church who are helping her get plugged in to programs that can help her with rent, job training, childcare, and more. One woman at our church works at a private Christian school in the neighborhood and helped get two of the children into the school. Another woman who teaches ESL courses is tutoring this mother so she can pass her high school equivalency test. Still another mother with young kids visits with this woman once a week to talk, clean, shop, sort through clothes, or do whatever needs doing. The body of Christ has come around this woman, this member of the body, to strengthen her and keep her from falling. Not only is she being formed, but those who are walking with her are being formed as well.

This is really a two-way embrace: The woman who needs help has opened her arms to our church and allowed us to enter into her life. She has put the kingdom before her sense of independence, her pride, or her need to prove something to others. The church has opened its arms by accepting that none of us can travel through life alone. This woman's struggles are obvious, but they aren't unique. Our church has created an atmosphere where people don't need to meet certain criteria before they are welcomed and ministered to. She senses that she is loved simply because she is our sister.

Change Can Come from Within

Before we moved to Minnesota, we lived in the Chicago suburbs and attended a wonderful church called St. Barnabas. We'd been attending for a few months when one of the rectors asked us to help start a small group for people between the ages of eighteen and thirty-five. The rector sensed that the "Gen X" demographic was slipping through the cracks at the church and she wanted to do something about it. Along with our friend Eric, we helped coordinate what quickly became a thriving young adults group made up of singles, married couples, and couples with young children. Like the women's group at our current church, this mixing of people at various life stages offered a rich and irreplaceable experience.

There are a couple of important lessons here. The first is that too often the church creates programs and then waits for people to sign up, rather than seeing a need in the community and exploring ways to meet that need. The second lesson is that pastors and other church leaders can be wonderful instigators for change, but often the most successful ministries are those that arise organically out of the passions and desires of the people within the community.

The same is true for ministry opportunities for women. Rather than simply starting up a Bible study for mothers, churches need to see women as people with complex spiritual needs. Women need to be welcomed, encouraged, and invited to join in every aspect of life in the church (read: provide childcare for *everything!*). We need to have our spirituality taken seriously. Those of us who are mothers are certainly impacted by life with our children, but we are so much more and need to be treated as such. More importantly, we need to be asked what we need and allowed to explore a wide variety of faith formation opportunities.

Moms Need Each Other

As part of my survey, I asked women I know to forward the survey to women they knew. I got numerous responses from women who attend the same churches. The women from one particular church all raved about the mentoring they receive from older mothers in the church.

One woman wrote, "The pastor's wife has spent countless hours sharing with me her own experiences and failures to spur me on to maturity in the Lord. My church allows me the freedom to make my own decisions and mistakes in the Lord. They care enough to be involved in my life and my children's lives so that we know how to pray for one another. They shed tears with me over my failures and rejoice with me in my victories." Another woman from this church wrote, "My sisters in Christ provide support when I need someone to watch my children. The people in our church really live 'laying down their lives for each other and having all things in common.' They are there at the drop of a hat."

Clearly, this church has tapped into a vital need in the lives of its women. It has created an atmosphere of openness, honesty, accountability, and trust that allows mothers to be themselves. The women in this church know they can turn to each other and be vulnerable about their needs. They are therefore free to be formed by the practice of mothering.

Mentoring is also a critical part of the ministry of MOPS. Carol Kuykendall, Director of Communications for MOPS International, notes that, while the focus of MOPS is ministry to the mothers of preschoolers by the mothers of preschoolers, mentor moms are essential for offering perspective and encouragement to MOPS moms. Kuykendall says, "She [the mentor mom] has survived. Her mere presence and encouragement gives moms hope that they too will survive these years."

Mentoring and other mom-to-mom connections are only possible if we are willing to be transparent about our experiences as mothers. Nearly every woman in my survey said she was surprised by the harsh realities of motherhood, that she never knew how hard—or how rewarding—it would be. And yet I don't think it's entirely possible for women who don't have children to understand what it feels like to be a mother, even if all the moms tell the truth about the ups and downs of raising children. The solution, then, is for us to be prepared with a safety net of acceptance, support, and honest empathy when the disillusionment kicks in. We need to pay attention to new moms and be on the lookout for the glazed "what-on-earth-is-happening-to-me" expression that comes with a lack of sleep and an excess of crying (from both baby and mama).

We need to be honest about our struggles and let other mothers know that they aren't alone in their sense of incompetence, their fears that they are messing up, their occasional dislike of their children. We need to help each other see God in the midst of our mothering, to guide each other down the paths God leads us on, even when our paths are different. We need to show each other how to live motherhood as a practice.

14

WHERE DO WE GO NOW?

Reimagining motherhood isn't just necessary for the well-being of Christian women, it is necessary for the well-being of the church as well. Because the cult of the family leaves little room for those who don't fit the mold, there are countless Christians who feel alienated from the church. Take my friend Natalie, who has struggled with infertility for years. "I feel defective when I sit in a church full of families," she tells me. Or Shelley, a single woman in her thirties, who says, "At the last church I attended, they simply didn't know what to do with single women once we were too old for the college group. The women's ministry was focused on mothers and had Bible studies at 10:00 a.m. on Tuesdays when the single women were all working. The utter lack of mention of singleness in sermons just showed that we were considered second-class citizens until we had gotten married." Or Jessica and her husband, Brian, who, because of their own deeply dysfunctional childhoods, aren't sure they want children, only to be told by people at their church that they are selfish and shallow. All of these women have wonderful gifts to offer the Christian community but are pushed out to the fringe of the evangelical culture because they can't be neatly tucked into the confines of its expectations.

The cult of the family has left women stressed out, depressed, and stripped of the joy that motherhood can bring. It has left the church bereft of the gifts of countless women who have either been shuttled off to raise children in isolation or told to wait until they have children to enter into the real life of the church. It has left Christian women—whether they are mothers or not—swirling in a state of incompletion: Without children, they are not wholly who God wants them to be; with them, they are relegated to a supporting role where their sole function is to develop their children. Worst of all, the cult of the family has pulled our focus away from God's call that we live lives of compassion, mercy, justice, and love and put it squarely on the small universe that is the family.

In the contemporary church, the ways in which motherhood impacts women have been shoved aside. Instead, motherhood has become all about raising children, about doing what's best for our kids. Even the more recent calls for women to take better care of themselves spiritually and emotionally are couched in terms of refueling us so we can continue to give to our children; it's good for us because it's good for them.

Think of yourself from God's perspective for a moment. In spiritual terms, you are still a child. You are not yet a complete creation with nothing left to learn; you are still in the process of being formed. Certainly the church would never suggest that once we have children we women are somehow done growing, or ought to take a break from our own spiritual growth for the eighteen plus years we're raising kids. But in making the way we raise our children the primary focus of motherhood, the church has taken the work God can and will do in mothers out of the picture.

Understanding motherhood as a practice allows us to move toward a place where the family is a vital and sacred part of our life with God but not an essential element of faith. We can indeed be whole people without ever becoming parents—the Bible is full of saints who never raised a child. And yet in our parenting, we must allow God to work in us and through us, not only because it's good for our children but because it's good for us. When we live motherhood as a practice, we open ourselves to God's power to form us and grow us into the people we are created to be.

I feel as if I've spent the last thirteen chapters griping. I've gone around and around about the tone of these chapters, thinking I needed to soften my "voice" a bit and be more delicate in my approach so that I can gently persuade readers to see my point. And then I get to thinking that maybe it's okay to be crabby about these issues, that maybe it's time for Christian women to talk about how hurtful it is to have our vision restricted by rules that have nothing to do with God's call on us as Christians. So I've left the crabbiness in.

So while I might sound kind of ornery at times, my purpose isn't just to be a gadfly but to cast some light on the unreasonable and unbiblical expectations the church has heaped on the heads of women. This book is meant to pull back the curtain on the lives of real women, women who feel stifled, stuck, and stranded by the expectations of Christian motherhood. Most of all, it's meant to help the church move toward a new understanding of motherhood, one that more fully encompasses who women are as daughters of God.

My dream is that this book will become a starting point for women who feel stymied by the unspoken restrictions of their Christian communities. I hope that pastors will at least flip through it and realize that the discontented woman who comes in for counseling represents others who are experiencing the same feelings. But those are my dreams. Only time will tell if they move anywhere close to reality.

NOTES

Chapter 1: The Cult of the Family

1. To learn more about the connections between the evangelical view of motherhood and nineteeth-century culture, see Jan Lewis's essay, "Mother's Love: The Construction of an Emotion in Nineteenth Century America," in *Mothers and Motherhood: Readings in American History*, ed. Rima D. Apple and Janet Golden (Columbus: Ohio State University Press, 1997).

2. Gilbert Bilezikian, *Beyond Sex Roles* (Grand Rapids: Baker, 1985), 207–208.

3. Elaine Tyler May, *Homeward Bound: American Families in the Cold War Era* (New York: Basic Books, 1999), xv–xvii.

4. Ibid., xviii.

5. Ibid., 11.

6. Mary Stewart Van Leeuwen, *Gender and Grace* (Downers Grove: Inter-Varsity Press, 1991), 49.

7. J. Lee Grady, *10 Lies the Church Tells Women* (Lake Mary, Fla.: Charisma House, 2000), 156.

Chapter 2: The Good Christian Mother

1. Apple and Golden, *Mothers and Motherhood*, 54.

Chapter 3: The Making of a Myth

1. Apple and Golden, *Mothers and Motherhood*, 25.

2. See Laurel Thatcher Ulrich's *Good Wives: Image and Reality in the Lives of Women in Northern New England, 1650–1750* (New York: Vintage Books, 1982).

3. Apple and Golden, *Mothers and Motherhood*, 53.

4. Ibid., 31.

5. Ibid., 57.

6. Ibid., 60.

7. Ibid., 61.

8. Ibid., 62.

9. Ibid., 90.

10. Ibid., 91.

11. Ibid., 96.

12. See Nancy Pottisham Weiss, "Mother, the Invention of a Necessity: Dr. Benjamin Spock's Baby and Childcare," in *Growing Up in America: Children in Historical Perspective,* ed. N. Ray Hiner and Joseph M. Hawes (Chicago: University of Illinois Press, 1985), 283–303.

13. Ibid., 293.

Chapter 4: Mothering God's Way

1. In case you're interested, this altercation ended when I decided to go with "logical consequences" as my discipline tactic of choice. I told Emily that if she chose not to wear socks and boots, her feet were going to be cold. Now my girl is not one to concede defeat, so as we walked to the car, it didn't surprise me when she turned to me and said, "Mom, my feet aren't cold at all!"

2. See the Center for Effective Discipline website for more on these studies (stophitting.com).

3. See the preface in Roy Lessin's *Spanking, a Loving Discipline: Helpful and Practical Answers for Today's Parents* (Minneapolis: Bethany, 2002).

4. Michael P. Farris, *The Spiritual Power of a Mother* (Nashville: Broadman & Holman, 2003), 39.

5. Ibid., 38.

6. Margaret Lamberts Bendroth, "Fundamentalism and the Family: Gender, Culture, and the American Pro-Family Movement," in *Nothing Sacred: Women Respond to Religious Fundamentalism and Terror,* ed. Betsy Reed (New York: Thunder's Mouth Press/Nation Books, 2002), 272.

7. Ibid., 273.

Chapter 5: The Truth about Depression

1. I'm not crazy about my coworkers, my parents, or my friends knowing that I'm depressed. I like to be in control of that kind of information. But I'm taking a chance because this book is about being open and honest about our experiences as moms and that will, at times, demand that we become a little—or a lot—uncomfortable as we reveal ourselves to others. At the same time, I have told a few people what I'm going through, and I am blown away by the care and compassion these people have shown me. So far, no one has seemed to think less of me because of this. In fact, my confession has served to deepen those relationships to a place I've always longed for but never would have dared go before. I can't tell you how much those friends have meant to me. And by the way, Mom, it's not your fault.

2. Archibald Hart and Catherine Hart Weber, *Unveiling Depression in Women* (Grand Rapids: Revell, 2002), 18.

3. Ibid., 24.

4. Ibid.

5. The *Diagnostic and Statistical Manual of Mental Disorders,* fourth edition (Arlington, Va.: American Psychiatric Press, 2000).

6. Hart and Weber, *Unveiling Depression,* 20.

7. Ibid., 39.

8. I want to be clear that while I'm taking issue with the emotional norms of Minnesotans, I am truly, madly, deeply in love with my home state and my fellow natives. Please don't send me letters about this.

9. Apple and Golden, *Mothers and Motherhood*, 61.

10. Nancy Guthrie, *Holding On to Hope: A Pathway through Suffering to the Heart of God* (Wheaton, Ill.: Tyndale, 2002).

11. To find a MOPS group in your area, go to www.mops.org or call 1-800-929-1287.

Chapter 6: The Social Disconnect

1. Caryn Rubenstein, *The Sacrificial Mother* (New York: Hyperion, 1998), 13.

2. Ibid., 31.

3. For a full discussion of this view, see Van Leeuwen's book, *Gender and Grace*.

4. Van Leeuwen, *Gender and Grace*, 46.

5. For court documents and trial transcripts of the Andrea Yates trial please see courttv.com

6. Rubenstein, *The Sacrificial Mother*, 111.

7. I need to take this opportunity to brag about my husband, for whom I have never left a child-care instruction in our six years as parents. He cooks, he plays, he does baths and jammies and stories and songs and prayers and snuggles—often with more patience and creativity than I. I am writing this chapter in June and he will be completely in charge of the children for the majority of the summer until I'm finished with the book (thank heavens he's a teacher with the summers off). He is definitely in the top 3 percent of dads.

8. Van Leeuwen, *Gender and Grace*, 40.

9. Bendroth, "Fundamentalism and the Family," 260.

10. Ibid., 267.

11. Ibid., 368.

12. Van Leeuwen, *Gender and Grace*, 36.

Chapter 7: The Stay-at-Home Mother

1. Van Leeuwen, *Gender and Grace*, 37–38.

2. Bendroth, "Fundamentalism and the Family," 266.

3. Grady, *10 Lies the Church Tells Women*, 160. Grady's chapter on women working outside the home offers a more comprehensive hermeneutic of Paul's commands about women and family life.

4. See Ann Crittenden's book *The Price of Motherhood* for an excellent explanation of the economic toll stay-at-home motherhood takes on women and children, not just in the short term but in the long term. Staying at home leaves women and children extremely vulnerable to poverty should anything happen to the primary breadwinner. And when poverty strikes, the entire national economy takes a hit.

Chapter 8: The Real Life of an At-Home Mother

1. Debra Bendis, "Intruder in My Arms," *The Christian Century*, April 19, 2003, 31.

Chapter 9: The Working Mother

1. See editor's note accompanying Proverbs 31 in the *Quest Study Bible* (Grand Rapids: Zondervan, 1994).

Chapter 10: The Real Life of a Working Mother

1. We have gained an invaluable knowledge of saving money from Amy Dycyzyn's *Tightwad Gazette* books (New York: Random, 1998). If you want to reduce your living expenses significantly, she's the one to show you how.
2. From Lisa Jackson's interview with Mary Whelchel in *Christian Parenting Today*, Sept/Oct 1999, vol. 11, no. 7, 46.

Chapter 11: Christian Motherhood Revisited

1. Alasdair MacIntyre, *After Virtue* (Notre Dame, Ind.: University of Notre Dame Press, 1984), 187. Please note that my explanation of a practice is a drastically simplified version of MacIntyre's and is undoubtedly flawed from a philosophical perspective. Any holes in the theory as presented are mine, not his.
2. Christian D. Kettler and Todd H. Speidell, eds, *Incarnational Ministry: The Presence of Christ in Church, Society, and Family* (Colorado Springs: Helmers & Howard, 1990), 220.
3. Bilezikian, *Beyond Sex Roles*, 15–16.
4. Grady, *10 Lies*, 26.
5. Bilezikian, *Beyond Sex Roles*, 36–37. If you're not buying this, or if you want a better understanding of Bilezikian's understanding of women and gender issues in the Bible, it is absolutely worth your time to dig into this book.
6. Van Leeuwen, *Gender and Grace*, 41–42.
7. Janna Malamud Smith, *A Potent Spell* (New York: Houghton Mifflin, 2003), 167.
8. Bilezikian, *Beyond Sex Roles*, 208.

Chapter 12: Practicing Motherhood

1. MacIntyre, *After Virtue*, 187.
2. Cameron Lee, in *Incarnational Ministry*, 309.
3. Smith, *A Potent Spell*, 24.
4. I have blatantly stolen this idea from my pastor, Doug Pagitt.

Acknowledgments

It's tempting to use this space to thank everyone I've ever known. And really, I should, because the people who have moved in and out of my life have shaped me in ways I am only beginning to understand. But since I am my mother's daughter and never met a stranger, I have to narrow the list down to a few who made it possible for my scattered ideas to become a book.

For starters, thanks to Camerin Courtney, Connie Neal, and Ed Gilbreath for making me form my premise out loud; to Ginger Kolbaba for getting the ball rolling; to Julianna Gustafson for being gracious and for getting excited about these ideas; to Lauren Winner for saying, "Yes, that's a book"; to Brian Peterson for listening to Ginger and taking a chance on me; and to the editorial and design teams at Baker for your patience with an opinionated editor.

Thanks to Mary Elizabeth Grosscup for guiding me through a year of tremendous change.

I also have to thank Pat McCarty, Gregg Muilenburg, George Larson, the late Ralph Hoppe, Nancey Murphy, Rob Banks, and Ray Anderson, teachers and professors who showed me how to think and write, but also how to look for God in the world.

Thanks also to Chris Lutes, Mark Moring, Marilyn Roe, and Harold Smith who turned me into an editor. And thanks to Mickey Maudlin for being a phenomenal mentor and an even better friend.

To Alan, Judy, Katie, Maggie, and the rest of the Sisters' Sludge staff, thanks for letting me loiter at the table by the window and for serving granitas into October.

To all the women who shared their stories with me, your honesty and willingness to pull back the veil on Christian motherhood has been a gift to me. I am confident God will use your stories to heal the hearts of your sisters.

Our community at Solomon's Porch—especially the Pagitts, the Colleens, the Thom, the Rachel, the Paris family and our Friday night group—thank you for letting me try out my ideas on you, for shaping my beliefs, and for playing with the kinder so I could get this thing done.

Thanks to my mom and dad for having an outlet in the porch so I could at least see the lake, for feeding my family meatballs, for not freaking out about chapter 5, and for your unwavering belief in my ability to make something of myself. You have practiced your parenting with excellence. And to my brother, Paul, the next book is all about you, man.

And then there's Anna Denman. My dear friend, you have raised my children during this process and I can never, ever thank you enough for that. Thanks for listening to me spout my theories about life, and for being the most extraordinary babysitter (not even close to being the right word) I could have asked for. You are an incredible woman, and I am honored to have you as a friend.

Finally, to my family. Jimmy, you helped me mold my ideas into something coherent and took over the parenting so I could write them down. You have no idea how much you have formed me. Emily and Isaac, you are extraordinary if I do say so myself. I am so very, very blessed to be your mom.

Carla Barnhill (M.A., University of Edinburgh) has served as an editor for *Campus Life,* the *Teen Devotional Bible,* and *Raising Your Teen without Losing Your Mind.* She has been published in *Books and Culture* and *Christianity Today* and received a Gold Medallion Award for *Blessings Every Day.* She is currently the editor of *Christian Parenting Today* and the mother of two children.